You will never read a more interesting book about how outsiders view the church. Overhearing the conversations between Jim and Casper as they go to church is pure gold. It's like being a reporter who somehow wound up in the White House and overheard the most private workings of government . . . and then got to use the information to help thousands of people. Jim and Casper will help any church leader who pays attention.

TODD HUNTER

National Director, Alpha USA
Former National Director, Vineyard Churches USA

Jim Henderson is one of the most creative, committed, insightful, honest, affable, and downright interesting people I've met. That makes me want to hear what he says and read what he writes.

BRIAN D. McLAREN

Author and Activist

Jim and Casper Go to Church is a daring book, way overdue. Jim and Casper call us to listen, to carry on a conversation, and to be honest and open— seekers of truth. This is not just a novel idea. It is exactly what Jesus did. We must begin talking to each other about the deep things that matter, the truths that call out for each heart and soul to be discovered, embraced, and known. *Jim and Casper Go to Church* is an absolute must-read for every pastor, staff member, leader, and person who takes expanding the Kingdom of God in a dark and hopeless world seriously.

DR. DAVID FOSTER

Author of A Renegade's Guide to God
Founding Pastor of TheGatheringNashville.com

I would like to dedicate this book to Helen Mildenhall, Christine Wicker, and Matt Casper, none of whom would call themselves Christians, but their kindness and courage have helped me to understand God in new ways.

Jim Henderson
Seattle, Washington

I dedicate this book to its readers: thank you.

Matt Casper
In San Diego and in a NY state of mind

JIM HENDERSON
& MATT CASPER

A believer, an atheist, an unlikely friendship . . .

JIM & CASPER
GO TO CHURCH

Frank conversation about faith, churches, and well-meaning Christians

BARNA

AN IMPRINT OF TYNDALE HOUSE PUBLISHERS, INC.

Visit Tyndale online at www.tyndale.com.

Visit Jim Henderson online at jimhendersonpresents.com.

TYNDALE is a registered trademark of Tyndale House Publishers, Inc.

Barna and the Barna logo are trademarks of George Barna.

BarnaBooks is an imprint of Tyndale House Publishers, Inc.

Jim and Casper Go to Church: Frank Conversation about Faith, Churches, and Well-Meaning Christians

Designed by Stephen Vosloo

Library of Congress Cataloging-in-Publication Data

Henderson, Jim, date.
  Jim and Casper go to church : frank conversation about faith, churches, and well-meaning Christians / Jim Henderson and Matt Casper.
     p. cm.
  ISBN 978-1-4143-1331-3 (hc)
  1. Church. 2. Evangelistic work. 3. Non-church-affiliated people. 4. Evangelistic work—United States. 5. Non-church-affiliated people—United States. 6. United States—Religious life and customs. I. Casper, Matt. II. Title.

  BV640.H46 2007
  277.3′083—dc22   2006101300

ISBN 978-1-4143-5858-1 (sc)

Printed in the United States of America

18   17   16   15   14   13   12
 7   6   5   4   3   2   1

CONTENTS

Foreword by George Barna vii

Introduction xiii
I Pay People to Go to Church

Rick Warren's Church 1
Saddleback

Church, L.A. Style 13
Dream Center

The Mayan and McManus 25
Mosaic

Mega in the Midwest .37
Willow Creek

Helen, the Almost-an-Atheist,
Takes Us to Church 49
First Presbyterian

Big Church or Church Big 61
Lawndale

The Drummer's Church 73
Jason's House

Emerging Church Weekend 87
Imago and Mars

Come as You *Really* Are 105
The Bridge

Osteen Live! 117
Lakewood

Keeping It Real 131
The Potter's House

Is This What Jesus Told
You Guys to Do? 147

Casper's Closing Words 153

Q&A with Jim and Casper 155

FOREWORD
By George Barna

Do you remember the first time you went to church?

When I was young, I frequented church, growing up Catholic. But, like so many other Americans, I dropped out for a while after college. When we got married, my wife and I went on what she called our "search for God" and gained exposure to a variety of Protestant churches. It was the first time I witnessed any expressions of faith outside of the Catholic tradition. Those visits to Protestant churches, which ranged from large, African American Pentecostal churches to tiny, middle-class, white fundamentalist congregations, shook us up. Our reactions spanned the gamut—from bored to mesmerized and repulsed to comfortable. After a few false starts, my wife and I wound up in a series of churches that led us to Christ and a more holistic Christian life.

But many people never have a positive church experience, or perhaps any church experience at all. Still others are jettisoned from the church world by hurtful or irrelevant experiences they suffer in those places.

In fact, even though many people think of the United States as a Christian nation, and journalists proclaim America to be "the most religious nation on earth," an enormous number of Americans—one-third of all adults—are unchurched. In part, that figure remains prolific because of the large number of young people who abandon the organized church as soon as they are no longer held responsible for their daily choices by their family of origin.

Historically, Americans have been attracted to Christian churches. Why the seemingly sudden change in behavior? It certainly is not because of a lack of churches: There are more than 335,000 Christian churches in this country. It cannot be attributed to the indifference of church leaders, since the primary measure of "success" used by churches is the weekly attendance figure. And it is not because church leaders are unaware of the existence of unchurched people: Best-selling Christian books trumpet the fact; well-attended seminars discuss methods of reaching the unchurched, and churches spend millions of dollars every year attempting to attract people who are not connected to a faith community.

Research among those who avoid churches suggests that the main obstacle is the busyness of these people. But that excuse is probably just a smoke screen; after all, churchgoing folks are busy, too. Somehow, despite equally frenetic schedules, churched people find a way to make time for church. Further exploration shows that people avoid church because they perceive church life as irrelevant, they have vivid memories of bad personal experiences with churches, they feel unwelcome at churches, or they lack a sense of urgency or importance regarding church life.

A Changing Environment

As our society changes, so do the reasons for the growing number of church dropouts and church avoiders. For instance, the encroachment of postmodern thinking over the past two decades has laid a foundation for new thinking about the value of skipping church. Postmodernism suggests that there may or may not be a supreme deity; each person must determine that independently, and that decision cannot be imposed on other people. According to postmodern thinking, how one chooses to handle that determination is a personal, private matter that need not have substantial influence on one's life. What matters most is that people are comfortable with their own decisions, and that they are able to have whatever faith-oriented experiences they desire.

Add to that the changing nature of the church scene, and things get even more confusing. Specifically, a growing number of Americans are shifting away from conventional church experiences and gravitating toward alternative expressions of faith. For instance, the recent jump in house-church involvement and the growing experimentation with online faith experiences are reshaping the field of options that are available. Gone are the days when it was a simple decision: Either attend the church on the corner or find a nearby congregation of your chosen denominational affiliation. In the land of choice, even the church world now offers people a veritable menu from which to select the best or most appealing option.

Finally, consider the fact that few religious leaders or churches have any idea what it's like for an outsider to try to break into the holy huddle. Most churched people have been so immersed in the church world that they have completely lost touch with what it is like to come through the church door and try to fit into a place that has very distinct habits, language, goals, events, titles, architecture, traditions, expectations, and measurements.

A Visitor Enters the Building

In some ways, then, attracting people to a conventional church is a greater challenge than ever. And if a visitor *does* enter the building, then what? What do first-timers see? How are they treated? What are the central messages they glean? How do they process the experience? On what basis do they decide whether or not to return?

That's what this book is all about. You are about to read the adventure of Jim (Henderson) and (Matt) Casper. This journey is the brainchild of Jim Henderson, a creative spiritual entrepreneur who has had a wealth of experience serving Christ from inside and outside the organized Church. You will be eavesdropping on a conversation between Jim, a committed Christian, and Casper, a committed but open-minded atheist. Like many good friends who want to share something of enduring value, they took a road trip—but in this case, their destination was churches! Casper gamely entered each of the churches Jim designated for the journey and agreed to describe his experience, akin to being a foreigner entering places unknown.

Marketers sometimes use a "mystery shopper"—an unannounced, anonymous observer, who is secretly sent into a client's environment to note what the experience is like for a typical outsider. In a sense, Casper was sent as a mystery shopper to examine the church environment in America. His articulate and insightful reactions within each church he visited should captivate the mind of every Christian who wants to make Jesus Christ more real and accessible to people. As someone for whom this whole "church thing" is new—someone who does not even believe that God exists—Casper brings a fresh pair of eyes to an environment that most of us can no longer see objectively. His reactions and observations are invaluable.

As you read his experiences, pay attention to the different axes on which he reflected:

- What is, and how compelling is, the call to action?
- How is the Word of God integrated into practical examples of living the faith?
- What prior knowledge and belief does the church assume attenders possess?

- Is the church more interested in conversation or conversion? In dialogue or debate?
- How accessible is the heart and mind of the ministry?
- Is the church engaging people or performing for them?
- How realistic is the teaching? Is it the result of proof-texting or contextualization?
- What is the church's capacity for listening?
- Is this a body of believers who are more interested in serving or in being served?
- What makes a church genuine and authentic in its interaction with people?
- How honest are Christians in discussing the cost of following Christ?

Those who have eyes to see and ears to hear will learn much from this fascinating trip to a sample of the outposts of American Christianity. It is our hope that this foray into the thick of ministry methodology and practice will motivate you to reflect on the definition of true ministry, the purpose of the local church, the commitment we should have to reaching people, and the best ways we can remain consistent with Scripture while penetrating our culture. But, as Casper points out during this trek to the holy hot spots, it's not what you know but what you do with what you know that matters.

INTRODUCTION
I Pay People to Go to Church

I spent twenty-five years as a pastor feeling like a failure.

Using the conventional standards of measurement most pastors live with (buildings, budgets, and butts in seats, a.k.a. the Three *B*s), it was more than a feeling—it was *true*.

For the life of me, I couldn't figure out how to get people to come to my little church. I tried "seeker sensitivity," "servant evangelism," "cell church," and even becoming a "contagious Christian." Nothing worked.

I was ordained in 1977 after spending seven years in training in an independent Pentecostal church. No seminary or Bible school for me: Just go out there and do it for Jesus. We started our first church in a small town just north of Seattle that already had twenty-seven churches, but a multitude of churches has never stopped a dedicated Pentecostal from launching another one. We viewed most church people as needing our upgraded version of Christianity as badly as the unsaved.

Like Steve Martin in the movie *The Jerk*, I would later discover upon leaving my closed spiritual community that things weren't exactly as I had been led to believe. I thought I looked like everyone else, but my seven years in the group had made me into something of a religionist.

I had started on the path with Jesus but had come out on the other side of what is commonly called the discipleship process thinking more like a Pharisee—the exact group of people Jesus had most of his difficulties with. I call such people religionists: people who have bought the lie that Christianity is supposed to be in the religion business when a simple reading of the Gospels reflects nothing of the sort.

In fact, what Jesus talked about looked more like Habitat for Humanity or Alcoholics Anonymous—a grassroots movement with no official hierarchy but lots of leaders; no offerings, but enough money to get the job done. Jesus called it the Kingdom of God.

Like a sunrise, the lights started to go on for me when I began to meet some Christian leaders from the *other* groups: Baptists, charismatics, Christian Reformed, and lo and behold, even Catholics. I began to "fellowship" with them and even started to like and respect them.

As I've now come to understand, *when people like each other the rules change*. And I was no exception. Jesus began washing away the bigotry, biases, and spiritual pride I had developed while in training for my first ten years of Christianity. I wish I could say that my experience was unique, but after thirty years in the business and hundreds of conversations with disillusioned pastors and leaders, I know I'm not alone—not by a long shot.

We called what we did "church planting," but it was really more like starting our own pizza place or coffee shop. I was taught that in order to be successful in the church-planting business (or at least look the part), we needed a building, brochures, and a salary.

So I began recruiting young people into our group. I talked to them about Jesus and many of them "accepted him as their personal Savior." All of that was good, but then I began turning them into better citizens. I began civilizing them the way I had been civilized.

That was not all bad, but it went much farther than I had

anticipated. In spite of my desire for people to encounter Jesus, I spent most of my time functioning as a moral policeman. (Young people can really test you in that area.)

In my first church, I had been taught that this was the church's primary task—being society's moral policemen—and that we should occupy ourselves with this task while we wait for Jesus to come back and rescue us from this sin-stained world. I even looked into joining up with the Moral Majority movement; that's how zealous I was. (Before I was saved I considered joining up with the Black Panther Party—stupidity has no favorites.)

I was so busy chasing the elusive Three *B*s of pastoral success that I hardly had time to focus on anything else. In fact, I outright ignored the people that Jesus himself primarily came to connect with—*the people Jesus misses the most.* (I say that Jesus misses them because a careful reading of the parables of the lost sheep and the lost coin in Luke 15 reveal that *God* was the one who felt the loss, not the sheep or the coin. Today, when people get lost we call them missing so that everyone will continue the search—calling them lost means all hope is gone.)

But thanks be to God! He saw to it that I struggled and stayed in touch with my humanity and failures. My wife, Barb, had a lot to do with that. She loved me and followed me—as did my three young kids—but never once did she buy into the "closed Christian community" line.

Fortunately for both of us, Barb had been theologically trained while serving as a Catholic nun for six years before we met. (Sorry, that story has to wait for the next book. But I did meet her while she was still in the convent.)

Barb kept reminding me that God is much bigger than I imagine, and that he is also kind to people who aren't interested in him.

I ignored her for a long time, but eventually I was worn down by her love and her authentic relationship with Jesus. This is in spite of the fact that she could never pinpoint the exact day and time that she "got saved," which was originally a sore point with me, but has now turned into a very humorous issue for us.

However, I really did love Jesus, so I never quit thinking about how to improve what we call church, and more specifically what we call evangelism. As I said, I was a complete failure at church planting (at least by today's megachurch standards), but like the player who spends a lot of time on the bench waiting to get in the game, I had plenty of time to ponder and pay attention to what we were doing and where we might be able to improve our approach to how we do church.

I ultimately decided that the one thing I could contribute to the church was to bring fresh imagination to the whole process of connecting with the people Jesus misses most—*the people formerly known as lost.*

It's said that desperation is the mother of invention, which probably explains why I eventually decided to pay people to come to church. That's right, I hired people—gave them cash—to come to my church. This may sound extreme, but bear with me.

We refer to what we do each Sunday as a service. We open our doors to the public and hope outsiders notice the Everybody Welcome! sign flickering in their peripheral vision as they speed by our building on their way to work, school, or play.

If we were in direct competition with other businesses, we would be considered part of the service sector. So wouldn't it make sense to mimic the practices of other businesses that regularly hire mystery shoppers or focus groups to help them better understand the needs of their prospects and customers?

If we really are providing a *service* to the public, why do we make such paltry efforts at trying to understand what they truly think? Why is it easier for us to spend millions on a building campaign than to spend twenty-five dollars on a one-person focus group to find out what he or she *truly thinks?*

I began thinking like this around 1994 when I read a little book called *The 22 Immutable Laws of Marketing.* I know this will sound sacrilegious to some, but I really felt like the Holy Spirit directed me to read that book and inspired me with certain specific passages.

The authors, Al Ries and Jack Trout, say that we expand our effectiveness by narrowing our focus. I realized that the church does not know what business we are in. Instead we practice what Ries and Trout call "line extension."

At a time long before the Internet revolution, Xerox, the famous copier company, attempted to go into the personal computer business. They reasoned that since they had succeeded in one business they could certainly succeed in another. In the process, they lost billions of dollars. That's line extension. They lost focus.

The church does this as well. Like Costco and Wal-Mart, we continually expand our offerings to our church attendees, hoping that they will see us as their one-stop "Mall for God." Most churches fail at it, but a few succeed, which is enough to keep the dream alive.

I knew I had to focus and, as mentioned, I was becoming painfully aware that it wouldn't be as the pastor of a megachurch. The only thing about the church's mission that captured my imagination was evangelism. By 1998, I knew that I would spend the remainder of my life trying to reinvent evangelism.

In addition to the book by Ries and Trout, much of my inspiration also came from a number of other business books I was reading at the time. I simply could not find any books written by Christians that were tough or pragmatic enough to help me break through to new thinking about old problems. Frankly, many of the authors on evangelism seemed as if they were playing *not to lose* instead of playing to win.

Since I was still pastoring a church, I realized that our resources would be more effectively allocated by focusing them on the people Jesus misses most. So I tried out a new, untested approach and started hiring unchurched people to attend services at twenty-five dollars per service.

The people I hired were the kind of people I wished would come to my church. The idea was to (1) pay them, (2) ask them to tell us how we could improve, and (3) pray that someone just like them would *voluntarily* come. Makes a lot of sense, doesn't it?

To make these people feel comfortable, I gave my unchurched/unsaved/lost visitors something official to do while they sat through the service—a survey. (This has since been refined and published as the Off The Map Church Survey, which you can find at http://www.churchrater.com.)

I instructed them that it would take about an hour and that they were not required to participate personally in the service (you know: sit down, stand up, kneel, sing, clap, *tithe*). They needed to understand that this was a real job, and I needed the survey completely filled out.

I also assured them that this would not be a bait and switch; I wasn't trying to trick them into attending another meeting. They were not prospects for conversion, nor were they obligated to return to the church: They were simply, well, *consultants*.

Heading Off The Map

I, too, was becoming a kind of consultant. In late 1998, after twenty-five years of being in *almost* full-time ministry, I resigned from being a pastor and went back to what I felt was more likely my real calling—painting houses.

I thought this was the end of my ministry career (did Jesus think of his work as a "ministry career"?). But between the time I resigned from pastoring and reinstated my contractor's license, I was offered a staff position as the director of evangelism at a large church.

I took the job because—like people who finish their graduate studies and then are offered a fellowship—I figured it was like being paid to do more research. Of course I didn't tell my new employer this, but God and I knew. I wanted to find out what a church that was committed to evangelism did when it came to getting ordinary people involved on a grassroots level.

I managed to survive the megachurch corporate culture for two years, and I enjoyed a great deal of the experience, especially the fine people I got to rub shoulders with. While there, I was asked to help produce a conference on evangelism. We called it "Evangelism Off The Map."

Because I was partially in charge of this event, I was able to try an idea that had been brewing in my mind for several years. I spend a fair amount of time in restaurants and coffee shops, and I often strike up casual conversations with the people who serve me.

Katrina was serving me coffee when I asked her if she'd mind answering some questions about spirituality. She agreed. Because she was a college student, she was used to the give and take of new ideas. Over the next couple of weeks, Katrina filled me in on all the details of her spiritual and church experiences. I eventually asked her if she would be willing to have this same conversation on stage in front of five hundred pastors. I said I'd pay her twenty-five dollars to do it. To my surprise, she said yes.

After finding two more like-minded people, we were ready to have our conversation, which I called "An Interview with Three Lost People." I had to explain to my non-Christian friends why we called them lost behind their backs, and I also had to ask their permission to use that term at the interview. They graciously agreed.

The objective was to create an opportunity—a face-to-face forum—for those who weren't "born again" to tell the "professionals" exactly what they did and didn't like about church, Christians, and Christianity.

Our "lost" friends' candor and humor caught the audience completely off guard—and they responded with a spontaneous standing ovation. My friend Dave Richards was in the audience, and based on the success and obvious impact our event had on the pastors at that conference, we formed the beginnings of what is today called Off The Map.

Off The Map helps Christians learn to communicate better with non-Christians, or as some of my more outspoken "lost" friends prefer to put it, Off The Map helps Christians learn how to not be jerks. From the very beginning, Off The Map has been working with (and often paying) people to tell us what they think about church and how we can improve what we call services.

I Bought a Soul on eBay

My friend Joe Myers, author of *Organic Community*, has been part of the Off The Map network from the beginning, and he knew about my odd hobby of hiring lost people to go to church. So he e-mailed me, assuming I would be interested in checking out an atheist who was selling his soul on eBay. He was right.

Hemant Mehta, a twenty-three-year-old graduate student at DePaul University in Chicago, was offering his atheistic attention to the highest bidder. He was tired of people pigeonholing atheists (sound familiar?) and was looking for a fun way to show that he could attend church with an open mind and give the speaker, the church, and the denomination their best shot at converting him. And he was doing it for a pretty cheap price as well—ten dollars per church service.

Much to his surprise, the bidding took off like a rocket. It soon reached four hundred dollars. I was new to the whole online auction process, so I called some friends who were experienced eBay bidders, and we formulated a strategy for winning the auction. We succeeded and won the auction with a bid of $504. Five hundred and four dollars for a man's immortal soul: *Quite a deal*, I thought.

With that $504, Off The Map had successfully bought our first soul. We promptly sent our new atheist staff member off to do what we had already been doing with other non-Christians—go to church and tell us what he saw.

Instead of fifty churches, I told Hemant we preferred for him to visit ten to twelve churches and to write about his experiences on our blog (an online discussion group you can find at http://www.off-the-map.org/atheist/). Word about our blog spread quickly, and soon fifty thousand people were consuming and/or contributing to the blog.

The *Wall Street Journal* religion reporter got wind of the story and flew to Chicago to attend the first church service with Hemant and me. The paper ran a front-page article on us that prompted a flurry of national and international media coverage.

For thirty days following the *WSJ* article, Hemant and I were on radio or TV every day doing interviews together. It was an honor to be given the opportunity to help people reimagine what it might mean for Christians to connect with non-Christians respectfully and authentically. Hemant felt the same way about his mission as well, which was (and still is) to put a new face on atheism. We essentially used each other to advance our two very different missions.

To be honest, I'd never given much thought to atheism or atheists. I always assumed that they were intellectual (mostly true), really into science (which I'm not), and, in general, pretty disgusted with Christians and church (again mostly true, but for reasons many Christians might find themselves agreeing with).

How I See the World

In my mind, humanity is divided into two groups: (1) people who follow Jesus, and (2) everybody else. It doesn't matter to me whether you call yourself a Christian, a Buddhist, a humanist, an agnostic, or an atheist. If you aren't following Jesus, you're in group two.

You might think that my including Christians on that list was a typo, but it wasn't. Jesus frequently—one could argue *always*—singled out "religious" people as examples of insincere or even fake followers. Think about his interactions with the Roman centurion, who was a hated terrorist in the minds of the Pharisees. Referring to this interaction with the centurion Jesus told the religionists, "I haven't seen *faith like this* in all Israel!" (Matthew 8:10, emphasis mine). He never referred to religious people in a similar fashion—ever.

The same is true today.

In my opinion, some professed Christians are not actually

following Jesus but are instead following religion. These people should more accurately be called religionists. Atheists are more honest about their unwillingness to follow Jesus, which is one reason I now enjoy interacting with them so much.

After the *Wall Street Journal* article came out, I began to get e-mails and phone calls from people all over the country. Some thanked me for what I had done, while others were appalled, offering comments like, "If you don't want to save his soul (for God's sake) give him my e-mail." This particular comment was provoked by a statement I made to the reporter that I don't hire atheists in order to convert them. Both Christians and secularists found this unbelievable, but I really meant it.

Keeping with that, I told Hemant that if he did happen to convert while surveying churches for Off The Map, it would have to be "off the clock." It wasn't that I didn't want him to follow Jesus (I did), but I wasn't going to use this experience to convert him.

Instead I was hiring him to help *convert Christians*, to provide us with the information we need in order to see how important it is for us to become more "normal" if we hope to truly connect with the people Jesus misses most.

To be honest, I don't really think of this as anything unusual. In my mind, I am just following the example the founder of our family business set when he used those we call *lost* to provoke those who call themselves *found*.

And when it comes to those Christians consider lost, who could possibly be more lost than an atheist?

Casper and I

We aren't called Off The Map for nothing. We invite people to travel to new places in their spiritual thought life and explore the margins where God is often secretly at work creating the next big idea.

After purchasing—or to be more accurate, *leasing*—a soul on eBay, I decided to head even further off the map. Hemant was offered an opportunity to write a book about his experience selling his soul on eBay. I decided to follow suit, but with a slightly humorous twist. Off The Map held a national contest to find an atheist who wanted to write a book with me, which is how I found the coauthor of this book, Matt Casper, or Casper for short.

You'll hear much more about this connection in a later chapter, but the short story goes like this: Some friends of mine in San Diego who lead what is called a missional community and have successfully blurred the lines between us (Christians) and them (non-Christians) got wind of our contest and told me I needed to audition their favorite atheist—Casper.

Casper is a copywriter, a husband, and a dad of two young kids. He is also a musician (or as he puts it, a "band guy") who writes songs about everything from dentists to deities. My friend Jason Evans, who leads the little community of Jesus followers I mentioned, also played drums in Casper's band, *Hell Yeah!* (That's the name of the band, not me swearing.)

Casper's dad is a retired teacher (whose workload included classes on contemporary religion, anthropology, and philosophy). He's also an atheist. His mother is a voice teacher and a singer, as well as a lifelong seeker of truth. She recently converted to Catholicism and currently leads the choir at her church. I flew down to San Diego to interview Casper and make sure he was really an atheist. How bad would it look if somewhere along the line he turned out to actually be an agnostic or, worse yet, a seeker? (We joked that he would need to sign a contract guaranteeing that he wouldn't become a Christian until three years after the book came out.) I was hoping that Casper, at thirty-seven, would bring a seasoned atheist's view to the book.

Casper's age, life experience, and willingness to explore the evangelical church experience with me was inspiring and energizing.

He told me, "Jim, like many atheists, I started out calling myself an agnostic. It sounds so much less, I don't know, *challenging*. But eventually, I realized that being an agnostic means you believe there's some sort of supernatural force at work in the world; you just don't know what it is. I didn't think there were any such forces at play in the world that I saw, and I realized atheist was a better tag."

As a young boy, Casper attended church, usually wherever his mother was singing. When it came time to attend college, Casper went to a Catholic university, "but I didn't really realize it was Catholic until I got there and wondered, *what's up with all the crosses?*

"I probably started to become an atheist in college. I saw a lot of people going to Mass, vespers, and all that. Then I'd see the same people making racist jokes, getting drunk and belligerent—but getting it all forgiven with a few Hail Marys. So I questioned the validity of their faith and, in turn, the validity of what I thought of as my faith."

Casper spent the late 1990s and early 2000s living in New York City. He and his wife were both working in New York on September 11, 2001. "I thought a lot about praying around that time, I can tell you that much," he told me, adding, "But, as we eventually learned, the people flying the jets into the buildings were praying too, so . . ."

Casper's wife was pregnant with their first child at the time, and they had already decided it was time to leave New York—9/11 just reinforced that decision—so they moved to San Diego, her hometown, in 2002.

By the way, there's a very funny Christian connection here, too. As fate would have it, Casper's first job in San Diego was working as a copywriter for Outreach Marketing, one of the top Christian marketing companies in America. I'm not sure how he got by their atheist/unbeliever scanner, but he did.

His job—coincidentally? providentially?—was writing those postcards churches hand out to unchurched people in an attempt to get them to come to church. "I figured that the day I wrote one that made me go to church, I would have reached my peak," Casper told me at one of our first meetings.

Casper left Outreach within a few months—"I just didn't fit, for obvious reasons"—but his time there did result in an authentic and unusual friendship with Jason, who, unbeknownst to Casper, was a pastor when not working at Outreach.

Casper calls Jason "my kind of Christian: He walks the walk, and his goal is not to convert me, but to be friends and play music— at least I think that's his goal. . . ."

When I first told Casper about the book, he was immediately onboard but with one condition: "I can do this, but I need *you* to be as open-minded with me as you need me to be with you, Jim."

"What do you mean?" I asked Casper.

"I'm currently an atheist, Jim. I say *currently* because I am open to the possibility that I may learn something that will change my point of view. Jim, can you say 'I am currently a Christian' and be as open-minded as me?"

I nodded. Yes. Let's write a book.

What to Expect from This Book

This is not a "tell me" book; this is a "show me" book. Casper and I spent the better part of the summer of 2006 traveling and visiting some of America's best- and least-known evangelical churches. We sometimes squeezed four churches into a weekend. We did most of our visits anonymously. The majority of churches we've included in this book have no idea that they are being featured. (Of course, we would love to hear from any of the churches we reviewed. You can post your thoughts for all to see at our blog: http://www.churchrater.com.)

This is the story of what happens when two guys with polar-opposite worldviews go to church together. As a Christian, I was overwhelmed by the experience of seeing something I took for granted, through the eyes of an atheist. It was simply life changing.

The church visits alone were eye opening. I think that once a month every pastor should send a group from his or her church to visit other churches anonymously. These people could then report back about what they think should change in their own church, based on what they've learned about how *not* to do church.

In this book, we devote one chapter to each church (except for "Emerging Church Weekend"). Each chapter tells our experience of "going to church." The chapters follow the chronology of our visits from beginning to end. We started at Saddleback in Orange County, California, and ended at the Potter's House in Dallas, Texas.

Because we had a limited amount of time and money (and both of us have day jobs), we had to squeeze in as many churches in the same geographical area as possible on each trip. And because the evangelical megachurches of America cast such a long shadow, we chose to focus primarily on those, as well as on some of the smaller, emerging churches that stand in that shadow. If we had the time and the money, Casper and I could have easily visited dozens, even hundreds of churches. (Maybe we can get to them all in the next book!)

With a few exceptions, we did not interview the pastors or seek out any leaders. We attended as visitors and reported our experiences as such. We only spoke to those people who approached us, and we did not seek anyone out for his or her opinion.

This book presents our personal views. It is not meant to be academically objective. Why? Because the people who visit churches are biased, subjective, and see church from a very limited perspective—mainly, what's in it for me? (To find out more about how people really feel about church and to leave your thoughts, visit http://www.churchrater.com.)

In a conversation that led up to the writing of this book, my friend Thom Black told me, "We don't need another book on defending the faith; we need a book on defending the space."

What Thom was referring to is the sacred relational space that occurs when two people trust each other (particularly people who would normally not trust each other). Thom and I both believe that rather than learning how to become defenders of the faith, we should instead learn to become defenders of that space. Because when two people begin to trust each other, they can learn to like each other. And when that happens, the rules change—and then people change.

Defending the Space

In the fascinating book *The Evolution of Useful Things*, the authors describe the development of ordinary objects like the paper clip, the fork, and the two-liter plastic Pepsi bottle. Although the subjects are common, the authors' conclusions are profound. My favorite lesson from the book goes something like this: *Hidden in every new idea are the seeds of its demise.*

For example, the aforementioned plastic Pepsi bottle. When glass bottles were new, they were all the rage. As their usage spread, the limitations of glass spread as well—mostly all over the floor. Plastic was already in use, but no one could figure out how to shape it into a bottle. After many false starts, the son of Andrew Wyeth (the famous American artist) eventually developed the plastic bottle. It was a boon to the soft drink industry, and sales took off. This was the early 1970s, and *biodegradable* was still a foreign word.

Maybe you can see where I'm going. The glass bottle was at one time an incredible innovation and a life-changing invention. However, due to its hidden drawbacks, that glass bottle would eventually be superseded by its plastic offspring. And today in our environmentally friendly world, we've learned that plastic bottles are just as susceptible to being replaced. Because *hidden in every new idea are the seeds of its demise.*

Evidence That *Demands* a Verdict

Following the turbulent and very liberal 1960s, evangelical Christians became determined to stand up for themselves culturally, politically, and evangelistically. It was time to come out and stand up for Jesus to be sure, but mostly it was time for Christianity and the church.

Since the mainline churches seemed determined to move away from proclaiming the gospel, the young evangelical movement saw an opportunity to differentiate itself in the marketplace of religious ideas. Consequently, a plethora of new evangelism ideas were offered by people like Billy Graham, Bill Bright, and others. Tools and programs like the Four Spiritual Laws and Evangelism Explosion—which reduced the amount of information a Christian needed to properly "present the gospel"—flooded Christian bookstores and church training programs. Whole new parachurch organizations emerged like the Navigators and Campus Crusade for Christ to carry the banner of this new evangelicalism.

As secularism continued to challenge what many saw as the Christian foundations of our nation, there seemed to be a need for a more thoughtful response. It was time for *Evidence That Demands a Verdict*, Josh McDowell's modern-day apologetic that "proved" Jesus really did rise from the dead, which in turn proved that Christianity is the one true religion. Lee Strobel, a convert from atheism to Christianity, would later weigh in with *The Case for Christ* and other best sellers that followed in the footsteps of McDowell's apologetic approach.

These authors provided Christians a way to *defend the faith*—the expectation being that if we provide a biblical response to the arguments of atheists or doubters and essentially prove them wrong, they will be forced to admit the error of their ways and join us. (Short of that, we will at least experience the pleasure of intellectually humiliating them.)

As a young believer, I read books like these and memorized phrases from them in hopes of being able to prove non-Christians wrong. I had a little more incentive than your average Christian as I had hopes of becoming a professional Christian (a pastor), so I really did need to know.

And here's where the seeds of demise come in.

Generally speaking, ordinary Christians don't like arguing their friends into becoming Christians. It just doesn't feel right. To be sure, we buy the books and really do want *someone* doing this kind of work. But the idea that we should *demand a verdict* from non-Christians seems like an approach a lawyer would take—and you know how people feel about lawyers.

Ordinary Christians like me know that when you start defending the faith, you also start losing your friends. On top of this, and largely due to evangelicalism's success in establishing itself as America's religion of choice, another cultural shift is occurring today. More and more Christians are tired of being perceived as mean, petty, demanding, and "right." For many of us, the only thing that attracts us to *apologetics* is that it sounds a lot like *apology*, which is what we actually feel more comfortable doing when trying to explain the church to our friends.

Practices, Not Principles

Jesus didn't just teach principles; he taught practices. He gave people something to do. He didn't just teach them about forgiveness; he told them to forgive their debtors. He didn't just talk about love as a concept (*eros*, *phileo*, and *agape*); he told people to love their enemies. He didn't just tell people to think about changing their behaviors; he told them to repent (change their actions). Sure it's challenging, but it doesn't take a weekend seminar to understand what he means.

As the teaching profession has risen to its place of primacy in the evangelical church, so also has the focus on principles . . . because that's how teachers think. With the proliferation of "The Principles of Everything You Would Ever Want to Know about Anything" seminars, it has become painfully obvious that what we need is not more information, but more formation. We need to learn once again to minor in principles and major in practices.

Those who enjoy defending the sacred relational space God has given them in their relationships with people have often developed a series of practices. These practices are attitudes that translate directly into actions. In fact, they often start in the opposite direction. We start practicing the practice even before we understand it or perhaps believe it, which often leads to surprising changes in us and in our relationships with people we normally wouldn't know how to relate to.

It might be something as simple as finding "conversation partners" from another faith or tradition outside of Christianity, people who can tell us why they choose their views over ours. It is also helpful to take turns telling these conversation partners what we find uncomfortable about our *own* beliefs.

Too often, conversations we have about our beliefs are too much like debates, and we spend our time looking for chinks in the conversational armor, spaces where we can insert an argument or launch a rejoinder. The practice of defending the space means *creating* and, obviously, defending such spaces. The practice of defending the space kicks in when we resist the urge to correct or attack and instead just listen (and maybe even take notes).

When learning something new (like riding a bike or parallel parking), the required movements feel awkward and counterintuitive. Under normal circumstances, we might even do the opposite of what we are being told to do. We have to practice the movements in order to make them part of our everyday lives, and we typically have someone running alongside of us for a while until we find our bearings.

Casper and I hope you'll feel that way about our story. We hope it will give you the confidence and the nudge you need to launch out into new relationships with people you may currently think of as ideological enemies.

When it comes to connecting with non-Christians, it seems that a few of us have learned how to defend the faith, while most of us practice the ancient art of doing nothing; for many, the maxim employed by Homer Simpson applies: "Trying is the first step toward failure."

Thankfully, as it does not require high levels of intellectual or verbal skills, even Homer could learn how to defend the space. Defending the space means *we protect our relationships with non-Christians*—they're real people to us, not targets. I think of it like this: They're just like me, except they're not currently interested in Jesus to the same degree I am.

Between various chapters, I will explain the change in attitudes and actions—the practice—required when shifting from defending the faith to defending the space. Look for shifts

- from apologetics to an apology
- from talking to listening
- from strength to weakness
- from beliefs to spirituality
- from debate to dialogue
- from manipulation to intentionality

RICK WARREN'S CHURCH
Saddleback

Casper and I drove north from San Diego on I-5. For our very first church visit, we were starting at (or near) the top, in Mission Viejo, California—the mecca of mega, the foremost outpost of contemporary Christianity. But most everyone calls it Saddleback.

Standing on the corner where Saddleback Drive meets Purpose Drive (yes, those are the actual street names), I kept Casper in my peripheral vision, checking for first impressions.

"I heard they let first-time visitors park up front," said Casper. "I also heard, though I doubt it's true, that if you're saved here you get a T-shirt. . . . Look at all these people. I feel like I'm at a football game or something."

"So, how does it feel to be standing at the vortex of evangelical innovation?" I asked.

"Vortex is right; I feel like I'm spinning a bit."

We parked our Saturn amid a sea of SUVs and joined the exodus of people moving from the parking lot to the pews. There were several giant white plastic tents on the edge of the parking lot. I told Casper that was where the kids, teens, and tweens enjoyed services.

"That's where they enjoy circuses?" Casper asked. I couldn't tell if he was joking or not since the circus was the only other place anyone but a Saddleback insider would expect to see tents this large.

And the tents were just the beginning. We saw movement and activity and signage everywhere we looked: carts wheeling past with pastries, fresh fruit, and bagels, and people, people, and more people, most of them headed toward a set of stairs lined with roses and divided by a waterfall spectacular enough to be located in the Mall of America.

I wasn't sure about Casper, but I have to admit I was already pretty much in awe of the whole experience, even though we were just barely past the parking lot. The size, the detail, and the campus were overwhelming.

Casper woke me out of my reverie. "Jim, look! It's a replica of Calvary on top of a replica of Jesus' tomb!"

We walked over and took a good look. I couldn't believe it. There really was an artificial replica of Jesus' tomb with a rock parked in the front door. It didn't look like it was a sacred shrine or anything, so we decided to try and roll away the faux stone from the faux tomb, but it was locked with a large bike lock and chain.

"Well, I hope they unlock it in time for Easter," Casper said. *I guess even Jesus' tomb isn't safe from vandals in Mission Viejo,* I thought, chuckling to myself.

Saddleback resembles something between a college campus and a theme park. It's a perfect testament to Southern California as well, with an outdoor café, outdoor seating, palm trees, and landscaping so manicured and perfect that it would make even Martha Stewart jealous.

As we ascended the steps beside the waterfall, I told Casper that this place got started on a credit card. Rick Warren got a five-thousand-dollar cash advance, bought some advertising, and went for it. The church spent the first part of its history meeting in plastic tents and got the first buildings up only recently.

"Wow, and now he's also like the best-selling author in the country, right?"

"Yeah, that's him, founder of Saddleback and author of *The Purpose-Driven Life,* one of the biggest sellers in history."

"Smiles everywhere. Good policy," said Casper while we made our way through an unusually happy gauntlet of greeters.

I silently wondered why we Christians seem to believe that it's our God-given duty to appear unusually happy—especially at church. I was beginning to suspect that taking an atheist to church could be an invaluable experience for all of us.

Casper and I shook hands with everyone who offered them, grabbed our programs (which Casper called brochures), and looked for a place to sit. We wanted a seat where we would be able to see everything but still work and talk quietly. We found a spot in the upper level and broke open our laptops, which attracted not just a few curious glances from our nearby fellow attendees.

We had a clear view of the stage and the two or three thousand people sitting down below. I asked Casper if he liked the view.

"It's awesome. I can see Nick Lachey from here. Well, it's not really Jessica Simpson's ex, but the guy singing looks an awful lot like him. That band is something else: rock star up front, fifteen-piece string section, six horns, background singers, and the ultimate boomer icon—the lead guitar player has a Les Paul guitar with the sunburst finish."

I told Casper we were going to play a little game called Rate a Church.

"I'll ask you to rate a few aspects of their performance today, using five stars like they do on TripAdvisor.com. Let's start with the music. On a scale of one to five, how do you rate the music?"

"Two stars," said Casper. "That's all I can do for you here."

I had been pretty impressed with the performance, so I asked him why he went so low. "They're world-class players, they're not missing a note, the singers are in tune, the music is upbeat, and they move seamlessly from one song to the next. What's missing?" I wondered.

"Well, yeah, for presentation and professionalism, they get a four or a five, but the music is too contrived, too slick, *too* professional, really."

"But that's a good thing, no? That should attract people, right?"

"Maybe people who like *American Idol*," Casper said with a smile. "I mean, don't get me wrong. I see the entertainment value, but when it comes to music, I like it pure. Too much polish and you lose the heartfelt power, you lose the soul of the music, and you're not gonna move anyone."

As I mentioned, Casper is not just a music fan; he is also a musician. His band frequently plays venues in and around San Diego. So when it comes to music, it's hard for him not to have a well-formed opinion.

Casper continued, "And the lyrics? 'Hope Changes Everything'? What does that mean? Hope changes nothing except your own feelings. *Action* changes everything."

Casper was taking his job seriously and really enjoying the imaginary microphone I was continually pushing in his direction. *Wow*, I thought. *We've only been in the building ten minutes, and the worship band and the music—what we Christians usually think of as one of the best ways to attract others to church—have been labeled contrived and soulless by Casper the Friendly Atheist.*

"Let's get into something more pertinent," I said. "What about the congregation, the people—what do you give them on a scale of one to five?"

"Well, it's pretty unfair to judge a roomful of people, but since you asked, they get a 2 as well, maybe a 2.5. I mean, they're paying attention and all, but based on some conversations we've overheard, I get the impression that this is something simply on most folks' schedules—Saturday: cookout. Sunday: church. . . .

"I mean, we're talking about God, heaven, the afterlife, the nature of existence, and the universe, right? And to me it feels like most of them are just watching TV, taking notes, paying attention to a lecture just as they would in school, but not really engaged in the spirit of it all.

"Case in point: The preacher asked everyone to 'greet the people around you.' Well, I don't mean to throw cold water on your church thing, but frankly, I thought that was lame. Why do you have to *tell people* to talk with each other anyway? Why didn't someone *voluntarily* approach me? 'Hi. Welcome to Saddleback.'

"Maybe if the church weren't so huge, there'd be a better chance to really connect with people. Is this what it's all about, Jim? Is contemporary Christianity driven by the 'bigger is better' maxim?"

"Don't know," I muttered.

Tom Holladay—a teaching pastor at Saddleback who sounds and looks like the actor Tom Skerrit (albeit a bald, shorter version)—took the stage. This guy was good: conversational, great timing, props, and lots of stories that were touching as well as personal.

I've heard a lot of preachers, and Tom was easy on the ears compared to many of them. He also did a great job of keeping people engaged without getting too loud or going overboard: a funny anecdote here, a verse there, a life story to tie it all together.

I was pretty sure that Casper would break out of the twos and get close to a four with him.

"So, let's play Rate a Preacher," I said. "I give Tom at least a 3.5, how about you?"

"I give him a two," Casper said, looking a little sheepish but knowing he needed to be honest if he hoped to keep his job.

"But what about the stories? Didn't his anecdotes and the way he kept the crowd engaged do anything for you?"

"Well, I guess maybe we should make a distinction between presentation and content, Jim. He's a real good presenter, but when it comes to relevant content—the meat of the matter, the words that give meaning to the obvious passion on display—I think he comes up a bit short. Tell you what: Since he included a real-life story or two—the one about his father coming to Christ being the most personal and moving—he gets a 2.5."

Casper was proving to be a tougher critic than I had originally thought. Here we were at Saddleback—the Super Bowl of churches—and we were only giving a 2.5. Looking for another angle to help bump Saddleback's average closer to a three, I asked a follow-up question. "You said you were moved, yet you still don't seem to be all that enthused. What's missing for you?"

"Well, where is the call to action? The challenge to make this world a better place? Even when Tom told the story of his father coming to Christ, it was not about what his father did or how he emulated Jesus' example. The message was that you don't have to *do* anything. Just say a prayer, use the magic words, and you're in."

I imagined Jesus saying something like this, but not an atheist! I quickly ran through the Jesus movie I keep in my head—all the things he did and said in the Gospels blended together into one image—and I anxiously tried to recall one time when Jesus said, "Pray this prayer and you're in." I couldn't recall one clip where he did that.

"Are you saying that you would prefer that the pastor tell you directly what followers of Jesus are doing rather than what they believe? Would that be more interesting and compelling for you?"

"Exactly," he shot back. "*That's* what's missing for me."

"But you don't see the whole picture of this church. They're helping eradicate AIDS and helping people in the third world. I believe Rick Warren is in Africa right now, working on that exact thing," I said.

"I respect that; who wouldn't? But that's so far removed that probably the only way it touches most people's lives here is through some long-distance connection and maybe a percentage of their tithe. Where was the call to action for these people here? Why didn't Tom say something about that today?

"If I did believe in God, and that I was going to be granted eternal life in heaven, I would want to do something significant here on Earth, to live as much of my life as I could following the example set by Jesus when he was here on Earth—do unto others as you would have them do unto you—I don't know, maybe I don't know the real story of Jesus. . . ." Casper's voice trailed off, but his question was stuck in my head. This conversation was quickly turning personal, and I knew Casper actually *did* have a relatively clear understanding of Jesus' message. As a veteran Christian, I was quite familiar with the checkered history of our movement and had spent the last thirty years thinking about why it sometimes feels broken to me as well.

I tried to explain. "A while back (1,700 years to be exact) the church drifted into the religion business. I call it beliefism—the worship of the right beliefs—and what you're hearing today is a version of beliefism. Rather than Christians giving priority to *what we do*, we've been taught a view that tells us what's really important to be known for is *what we believe*. Does that make sense?"

"I think I see what you mean, Jim. Based on what we've seen today anyway, the emphasis seems to be on simply *believing*. But does believing fix or change anything? I mean, the theme of today's sermon was 'don't give up.' Don't give up? Don't give up what? Don't give up coming to church? Don't give up believing in God?"

"Right," I agreed. "That's the basic offer the church makes to the marketplace. We tell people that they will find hope and life if they choose to believe in Jesus. Basically we say that our beliefs are better than the beliefs other religions are offering."

"I get it, but here's where it starts to feel unreal to me," said Casper. "The pastor kept talking about the problems the people in this church are probably facing in their lives . . . and yeah, we've all got problems. But we're sitting here in Mission Viejo, California. Half these people are probably worth a few million apiece, based on the cars and clothes I've seen today. I mean, how bad off can you really *be* here?

"Why the unrelenting focus on 'don't give up' for an audience that, when compared to the rest of the world, practically has it all already? The sermon stuck with telling people that their main objective is dealing with their own struggles, which are what? Crises of faith? Cash flow? Relationships? I know it's not about having enough to eat or a place to sleep tonight.

"I don't mean to be overly critical, but what if instead of asking people to pray a prayer in order to get into heaven, the pastor challenged everyone to go out and serve someone else here on Earth? Could you imagine if he told everyone here today to go out and make a difference *today*—donate two hours of their time at the local shelter, buy a new set of clothes for a homeless person; can you imagine what a difference that would make in one day alone? Maybe he'll cover it in another message."

The service was ending, and someone asked us, "Are you guys spies?"

We turned around and met Randi, a young guy from India who was intrigued by all of our typing and wanted to know what we were up to. Randi would turn out to be the only person who spontaneously approached us the whole time we were on the campus at Saddleback.

"We're writing a book," Casper said, shaking hands with him.

"He's an atheist and I'm a Christian," I explained.

"Really!" Randi said, looking at Casper as if he had just sprouted another head. "I used to be an atheist as well, but mostly I was a Hindu."

"Hindu? So were you really an *atheist*, or just non-Christian? I mean, as a Hindu you had a spiritual framework; you believed in an afterlife of some kind, a higher power, right?" asked Casper.

"Well, yes," said Randi. "I was a Hindu, but I was looking for a way out of the endless trap of the caste system. My father told me that only one out of a billion make it to heaven and that most of us have to live multiple lives [be reincarnated] and over time become Brahmans before we can escape our caste. It takes thousands of life cycles.

"When I moved here and got a job as a computer engineer, I came to this church and heard that anyone can get into heaven if he or she believes in Jesus. If that is the case, I said, then I am a Christian, and you know what? I really have found happiness here in this place with these people."

"Wow." Casper seemed genuinely moved by his story. "I was

about to say it sounds kind of like you were switching health plans—Hinduism offers complete coverage after thousands of years, but Christianity offers salvation the first time around. It sounds like a step up for you."

Randi said it was more than that. When he came to Saddleback, he found a place where he truly felt he belonged, and that had as much to do with his coming to Christ as it did with simply coming here and being around all these people who feel the same way.

We said good-bye to Randi and began to wind our way through the Saddleback Mall. A whole new group filled the church as we walked down the steps and past the waterfall, the artificial tomb, the artificial Calvary, and the sea of SUVs, toward our car.

We stopped at a nearby café to review what we had just experienced and go a little deeper. I got out my laptop and asked Casper if there was anything that he admired about Saddleback.

"This may sound strange, but I admire their ability to target. I'm a marketer, so I know a thing or two about this. Rock music for the kids, more casual services for the young adults. I even saw this targeting in the wide range of options they offer their congregation: help for those in recovery, help for relationships, and so on. I think the next step would be to proactively offer that same level of support to the public, the less fortunate."

"How about Pastor Tom's story about his dad coming to faith—did that move you?"

"Not so much. What moved me more was Randi's story."

"Why his story and not so much Tom's story?"

"Pretty simple. Randi told his story, while Pastor Tom put on more of what I saw as a performance. It's really no contest. Randi was able to communicate more about what it means—to him, anyway—to be a Christian. And to my ears, that content creates a much more engaging story. Tom was, pardon the pun, preaching to the choir, which meant little to me."

I understood what Casper meant about truly engaging people with personal stories. I told him about how long I'd been in the church, and about my own struggles to make sense of it at times. I explained that in many ways, those struggles prompted me to write this book.

"Exactly," said Casper. "Faith is a choice, and no one feels that great about choices made under pressure."

He paused a bit. "What about you?" he asked. "How did you find faith? Is faith something in your family? Did your parents have faith? Do your kids?"

Over a cup of coffee or two, I shared my story about how God encountered me, what I've done about it, and how my experiences with Jesus motivate me to keep trying to follow him and live a life that is real.

As we left the coffee shop, Casper turned to me. "You want to know what moved me the most today?"

"Let me guess: the faux tomb/Calvary combination? The waterfall with flowers?"

"Close, but no cigar. What really moved me was talking over coffee with you."

I was caught off guard by his transparency, but I understood what he meant. Casper and I were not just business colleagues; in a short time, we were beginning to enjoy and actually trust each other. Telling me that he or she trusts me is the highest compliment a non-Christian can pay me, and I felt humbled.

"Jim, if a complete stranger comes up to me and starts professing his faith, it's easy—*too* easy—to say that dude's nuts. But when people take the time to tell me about themselves, give me some context for their story, give me names, places, and times, it makes more sense.

"A lot of times, people claim they've heard God talk to them, and I usually think, *This guy hears voices.* But don't worry; I don't feel that way about you!"

I was glad Casper and I were getting to know each other. And I was glad he didn't think I was nuts. I didn't think he was either. And I told him so.

CHURCH, L.A. STYLE
Dream Center

As we drove into the Echo Park neighborhood of Los Angeles, I told Casper a little about the history of Angelus Temple, a.k.a. the Dream Center, and its famous founder, Aimee Semple McPherson. ("That name rings a bell," he said.)

I was glad a bell was ringing for Casper, but I wondered how much he really knew about Angelus Temple. This place had grown out of one hundred years of very complex evangelical history that most Christians don't even know about. I tried to explain.

"A partially blind African American preacher named William Seymour came to L.A. in 1906, holding meetings near Azusa Street, where people began getting healed and speaking in tongues."

"Ah, speaking in tongues. I've seen a bit on TV. You probably know the guy—Robert Tilton. What a show that guy puts on!"

I let that ride as a fair-enough comparison, knowing that it was fruitless to explain the theological nuances of glossolalia.

"So, tongues, healing . . . what happened next on Azusa Street?" Casper asked.

"Well, the ministry expanded and more and more people—from the city and eventually from the suburbs as well—came to his meetings and 'got the Holy Ghost,' as they liked to call it."

"Yes, I believe he's a relative of the Casper family: Casper the Friendly . . ."

"Yes, Casper," I said. "That's funny." But I was on a roll now and wasn't going to let some cute atheistic humor throw me off.

"Eventually this movement touched a woman named Aimee Semple McPherson, who in 1923 built this church where the Dream Center now meets. She called it Angelus Temple, and she was *outrageous*. One time she even rode into the sanctuary on a motorcycle to attract attention to the church."

"What?"

"Listen, that's just the half of it. Aimee hated the sound of change clinking in the offering plate, so she was known to lower clotheslines down from the ceiling for people to pin dollar bills to.

"Aimee also tried to fake her own kidnapping so she could run off with her radio engineer. More than a month later, she 'miraculously' reappeared and was warmly greeted by her church upon her return.

"But out of her (very human, to say the least) leadership, a whole denomination has sprung up called the Foursquare Church, which now has thousands of churches as part of its network. And this church we're attending today is where it all began."

Then, we turned a corner. "Look, there it is!"

"Where? Is it next to that sports arena?"

"No, Cas. It *is* that sports arena."

"Cool," Casper said. "I like it already."

"Why's that?"

"Well, it's right here, in the heart of the city. Amidst the poor and suffering. To me, that makes more sense than building a campus out in the middle of nowhere. Put your church where people need it most. I also like the fact that there appears to be a very solid mix of people heading inside."

"This church is seriously multicultural," I said. "African American young people and a lot of Hispanics as well." This was the first time we'd seen this mix of ethnicities in church.

"You know what?" I said. "If the Dream Center had been in existence when I signed up with Jesus some thirty-five years ago, I probably would've gone to church here."

Casper asked me why.

"I started my Christian career in a seventies version of this kind of church. Hundreds of passionate young people fired up with revolutionary-like fervor gathered to pray, sing, shout, jump, and dance every Sunday."

"Yeah, and look at all these people. It's kind of like what we experienced in the parking lot at Saddleback, where thousands of people were all headed to the same destination. Except here, it feels like the people are a little more connected."

"What do you mean?"

"Well, it's like it's more organic; these people appear to be walking to church from their homes, not from their Hummers. They greet each other from across the street. It doesn't seem as much like a church service as it does a neighborhood event . . . at least from the outside."

"It's the Pentecostal Church vibe you're feeling," I explained.

"So will we see some healing and speaking in tongues today?"

"Let's see what happens," I said, hoping nothing too weird would take place, while the ghosts of my Pentecostal past whispered, why not?

We took seats in the balcony, where we'd be able to get a better view. Casper immediately picked up a scent unfamiliar to me.

"Wow! A fog machine—and check out that camera crane!"

"Where?"

"Right next to the laser lights on the left-hand side of the stage."

When the band took the stage, the house started rocking! The young musicians looked very sharp, not only in person but on the eight-by-ten stadiumlike projection screens.

Casper asked, "Is this Sunday morning or *Saturday Night Live*?"

I asked Casper what he thought about the music.

"Well, I find myself reflecting on my assumptions when I go see bands in clubs, and I wonder if they're applicable here."

I asked him to elaborate.

"Well, for instance, what goes on backstage? I doubt they're partying with groupies or anything. One, it's church, and two, it's Sunday morning; but then I think, we *are* in L.A."

I told him that when the band is backstage its members are probably praying for God to help them deliver a good worship service.

"Well, it looks like their prayers were answered. Everyone is pretty fired up."

"What do you think of the message in the music?" I asked.

"Kind of the same thing as we experienced at Saddleback, Jim: 'We will stand up and fight and leave this world someday.' Frankly, all the language about fighting makes me nervous. I understand I'm in church; I understand that everyone here worships Jesus; but the way they're saying his name over and over and over again, until it's just another word or—hey, are those guys ushers or bouncers?"

Casper pointed to a couple of heavyset guys standing near the stairs.

"They're ushers," I told him. "But they're also probably ex-cons—guys who would make good bouncers. I know this church pulls a lot of people from the community to do work here; they also work with people out of prison, giving them a hand up as it were."

"Well, I have nothing but respect for that . . . and for those huge guys, too."

The band started with about three up-tempo numbers and then segued into a raise-your-hands ballad.

"Get 'em fired up, then drop the ballad," said Casper.

And then it was time to meet the preacher.

"We're soooooo glad you're here today; something spectacular is going to happen to you, I just know it." It was Pastor Matthew Barnett, the thirtysomething pastor of the Dream Center who took the stage as the professionally prerecorded video announcements went to black.

"He kind of looks like Ryan Seacrest—or maybe that's just what I'm thinking because of the *American Idol* vibe of the band," said Casper. I was starting to see how much Casper and I were on the same page.

"Let's welcome the teams from Texas, Kansas, and Colorado," the pastor said.

"There are teams here?" asked Casper.

"Yeah, but not sports teams; these are teams of people who have come to volunteer to help with the Dream Center."

Pastor Matt then invited new visitors to explore the facilities, and even to use the gym.

"They have a gym?"

"Yeah, and they also have a lot of beds here to help the homeless and drug addicted."

"Wow," said Casper, appearing once more to be genuinely impressed. I could tell that this particular revelation addressed his ongoing concern for a call to action in the church. And it was about to get even better.

"And remember to come to church the rest of this week; we're hosting the L.A. Pastors' School," Pastor Matt exhorted. "You don't want to miss this week; it will be *the greatest week* of your life. We'll be taking pastors out on the street because that is the main thing they need. They've had enough success principles.

We're going to take them out to meet people on the street and to help kids who are poor. *That's* what changes pastors more than anything else: getting them out there on the streets and letting them share the blessing."

"That's a call to action!" said Casper. "He's talking about being on Hollywood Boulevard, helping people. The church is in a poor neighborhood, too, which is where Jesus would like it, right, Jim? This is closer to what I was looking for—some kind of call to action. These guys are actually helping people, and the diversity of the attendees seems to be pretty representative of the urban area where they are located.

"I can relate to this part of the church, but I don't understand why they need to do the big show. Why don't they just help people and call it good? Why the fog machine, camera crane, multiple screens, PowerPoint, and the lights, lights, lights?"

"Casper, look at all the young people," I said. "Do you think they would show up if there wasn't a big show?"

"Okay, but is that what Jesus told you guys to do? Put on a Christian rock show that's visually and sonically indistinguishable from a non-Christian rock show, change the words, and call it church? Is that pulled from the Bible?"

I had been wondering when Casper would get around to asking me about how Jesus was connected to church, but I didn't expect it quite so early in our project.

"Jesus didn't really say much of anything about how we ought to do church. He did talk a lot, however, about how to *be* the church, and what to *do*—like helping the less fortunate and those who are poor in spirit. But Casper (and this is going to probably come as a shock to you), as far as I understand it anyway, Jesus never intended for the institution we call Christianity to form into a religion."

"Jesus never meant for Christianity to become a *religion*?" Casper seemed truly surprised. "Jim, I've seen enough TV preachers to know that what you're saying is nothing short of heresy."

"Jesus mostly talked about the Kingdom of God coming to Earth, and he told his followers to pray for it to come to Earth just as it is in heaven. But he personally only mentions the word *church* twice."

"Hey, I'm not even a believer, yet I feel somehow inclined to burn you at the stake!"

I told Casper I appreciated the thought and the kind word, but that, as an atheist, his tongue-in-cheek outrage was misdirected since he is in even more trouble than a so-called heretic.

"Well, our *heresies* aside, I think the light show and all that, for me anyway, does less to attract and connect me than to disconnect me. But I'm still not convinced when you say that Christianity was not meant to be a religion. It's the biggest religion in America, right?"

I thought I could kill two birds with one stone here and explain to Casper that in reality, his view and mine were somewhat intertwined. "Jesus came to start a movement that would advance his mission of bringing reality, sanity, and love back to planet Earth. But, to make a very long story short—and remember, Casper, this is only one view of Christian history—this plan got hijacked early on by some religionists who managed to institutionalize the movement. The result of those efforts is largely what you and I have come to think of as Christianity.

"And not only that, Cas, but a lot of what happens at church is really just cultural stuff. Preachers don't usually call it that, but churches adapt to the culture they identify with and take on the communication style they feel most comfortable with. The Dream

Center is a hybrid of classic Pentecostalism mixed with L.A. street culture and ethnic diversity. It's Christianity, L.A. style."

"Interesting," said Casper. "Because I just heard the pastor tell how this church is 'not like *religious churches.* . . . We go out in the street; we work with the people.' And when he said that, I thought, *Well, explain the thousands of dollars spent on that camera crane alone. How does that help you work with people?* I can't really tell what this church stands for, Jim. Is it helping people or growing the organization? Is it a community or a religion?

"Each church seems to want to say how it's different, yet the basic show is the same: sing, preach, pray, collect money. Sure, the style, the way they go about doing it has a different feel, look, and sound in each place, but—again, speaking as an atheist—for one to have a connection to God seems so astounding in and of itself. Why give it such a formulaic treatment?"

"I hear you, Casper."

Our conversation was suddenly interrupted when Pastor Mike Rogers, who Casper pointed out had a "Larry the Cable Guy kind of aura," took the stage. His job was to deliver the call to offering, and he did it well.

"This world—our bills—tell us we're broke," said Mike. "But we gotta heed God's Word. I was in the hospital getting all kinds of bad news, but God said I was okay."

Then Pastor Mike paused dramatically, looked at the audience, and slowly asked, "Now, whose report you gonna believe?" The crowd went wild.

And then he said, plain and simple, "The reason God healed me was because I gave." And the buckets—literally white plastic two-gallon buckets—were passed. *I could use a couple of those on one of my painting jobs,* I thought.

"That's a pretty direct appeal, Jim. I mean, the guy basically said, 'Give money, and God rewards you.' No denying that logic."

I told Casper that in my experience, Pentecostals seemed to be especially committed to making that connection, and that it probably is more of a sociological function than a truly spiritual one.

"Care to expand on that one, Jim?"

I did. "Pentecostalism has grown over the past one hundred years primarily among the poor and socially marginalized. As that group matured they began to look for symbols of God's blessing. Money has always been on the table as a sign from God."

"I know I feel a bit better when I have money than when I don't," Casper interrupted.

"Exactly. Pentecostals appeal very directly to human needs and hold out the hope of a God who cares about the here and now, which may explain why it is not only the fastest growing segment of Christianity, but also the fastest growing social movement in human history, with over 100 million adherents."

After the offering was collected, Pastor Matt called some dads to the stage in honor of Father's Day. Most had stories about how God had granted them longevity and blessed them with healthy, happy children.

A nineteen-year-old dad told how he had come to Christ and quit drugs, and how his belief was affirmed when God used him to help a man walk again. The crowd took that story in stride with the others—but not Casper, the sharp-minded and on-duty atheist. Unaccustomed to the casual language Christians often use to discuss the supernatural, he was brought up short by this comment.

"Did he just say he healed someone who couldn't walk?"

"Yeah," I said.

"Well then, why in the world is he wasting time hanging out in this building? Doesn't he know that there are thousands of people in this city alone who need his touch? And why does this building have handicapped ramps if one of the congregants has the power to heal those who can't walk? How can people here just nod their heads to a story like that? To me, that is truly astounding! This man can heal people: Get out there, then! There are people who need your help!"

I took Casper's monologue into consideration. Here is something that we churchgoers often take for granted. But to nonbelievers, a comment like "God healed me" is on par with saying, "I grew wings and flew around the world." All I could say at the time was "Good point, Cas." Fortunately, Pastor Matt saved me from having to answer Casper's very complicated questions (I'm sure you know the feeling), and soon we were both back to taking notes on our laptops.

The sermon was about Father's Day and included seven challenges for fathers. They were:

1. Be patient. Don't be too demanding at home.
2. Be predictable. Be consistent in your behaviors with your family.
3. Be practical. Don't play favorites. (For this, he used the example of Joseph and his coat of many colors as an example of how *not* to be practical.)
4. Be present. Be home as much as possible. (He used the story of Chuck Swindoll Jr., who said his dad was "never there for him," explaining how the family suffers when a man puts religion before family.)

5. Be positive. Lift people up with your words, don't put them down. "Cursing is not bad words; it's saying bad things." (Casper said this *really* resonated with him.)
6. Be pliable. Your kids will not be copies of you, so be flexible with who they are.
7. Love life with your kids. Show them that life is bigger than their block, and that the biggest thrill in life is not Magic Mountain but serving God (though a surprise trip to Magic Mountain is in no way a bad thing).

As we walked to our car, I asked Casper about the sermon.

"I really liked it," he said, much to my surprise.

"Why did you like it?" I asked.

"Well, maybe he caught me on a good day—it is Father's Day after all, and I'm a dad myself. And the messages—rather, the challenges—he relayed were not entirely faith dependent. Some of this stuff I'm actually taking home with me."

"Was there anything you didn't like?"

"You know me, Jim: I'm always able to answer both sides of the question. I didn't like the way the pastor got choked up, as if on cue. It was almost a deal breaker for me. It seemed so contrived, so manipulative. I wondered, *Who is that stuff for? The congregants? Himself?* It's certainly not for first-time visitors like myself. But you know what I realized? The theatrical catch in his voice may be more about being in L.A. than being in church."

Defending the Space

From Apologetics to an Apology

In his best seller *Blue Like Jazz*, Donald Miller tells about setting up a confessional on the campus of Reed College. People would enter the confession booth intending to recount their sins, but before they could get started, a Christian would begin apologizing to them for all the sins the church had committed against them. This surprising action caught people completely off guard and instigated a whole new kind of relationship between a Christian and a person formerly known as lost.

Telling someone, "I'm sorry for the way Christians have misrepresented Christ" always surprises non-Christians. Frankly, most non-Christians have learned to see Christians as arrogant and unconcerned about their opinions. Offering an apology may in fact be the most effective way to get a conversation rolling. The old saying applies: People don't care how much you know until they first know how much you care.

Defending the space means we practice apologizing to non-Christians for the sins Christians have committed against them. We simply say something like, "I'm sorry that we've failed; that really doesn't look much like Jesus, does it?"

THE MAYAN AND McMANUS
Mosaic

A church like Mosaic *should* be in L.A. and *should* meet in the Mayan Theater. Hip, colorful, artsy, and edgy, Mosaic is a must for many emerging church types, and Erwin McManus is an emerging celebrity pastor. He's a prolific author and frequent guest speaker at large conferences all over the world.

"Hi, I'm Todd. Welcome to Mosaic." We were greeted personally (and genuinely) three times between the parking lot (Can you be sure to not park anyone in front of us since we may have to leave early to catch a flight? No problem!) and the lobby of the Mayan, which, when it's not being used by Erwin, is a nightclub. I saw Casper smiling.

"What's up?" I asked.

"Well, this is the first, um, facility we've attended where I feel a sense of recognition upon walking in, like, 'Ah, I know where I am: a bar.'"

An easygoing guy named Keith greeted us in the lobby, which was dark with lots of purple material draped along the wall like those retro theaters from the forties. He told us that they purposely decided not to have a fixed location since that would tie them to a place they then would have to worry about more than the work at hand.

He also told us that they got here early to clean the vomit and beer off the floor from the night before—when it was a bar. It was hard to imagine this place less than twenty-four hours earlier, filled with hundreds of most likely drunk young people rocking to another we-want-to-be-famous L.A. band.

I told Casper that I thought these guys at Mosaic were the best yet at the uncontrived greeting thing.

"I know; they already have a five from me in that category, Jim, but there's still some kind of HR-staff, Wal-Mart-greeter friendliness about it all. Like this is their job, being nice to people."

"Well, when you think about it, that's exactly their job," I told him.

"Job or no, they're good. The five sticks," Casper said, all the while trying to manage the special notices people were shoving at us: information on the Mosaic gym, notices for three different Mosaic locations, a pamphlet on "The Controversial Jesus." And all this was happening in front of a huge stand of McManus's books and other merchandise, which was located just up the stairs from the main entrance, next to the well-appointed espresso bar stocked with lattes, scones, muffins, and all things Starbucks-like.

So, a quick update: We'd been greeted by no less than a half dozen fresh-faced teens and tweens; we'd had at least three people see to it that our car would not get boxed in; we'd passed a "Starbucks"; we'd seen about a dozen books for sale; and we'd learned why Mosaic did not have a fixed location—and we had yet to make it past the lobby area into the main auditorium, which beckoned like a colorful, psychedelic painting through the doorway.

Keith, stood by, letting us soak it all in. He was probably about twenty-five or so, with that healthy, sun-scrubbed look of the SoCal native—the "crunchy surfer look," as Casper said later.

"Hey, Keith, what brought you to Mosaic?" Casper asked, trying not to get distracted by the band setting up under muted lights on the main stage.

"I came here a couple of years ago and it just worked for me. I used to go to church as a kid, and my parents were sort of nominal churchgoers, but once I went to college, I moved away from all that. One night, a friend of mine said I might want to check out Mosaic. And I did. I came here and really connected with the community and then with God. I just graduated from USC last month and start a new job this week."

"Hey, congratulations," I said, thinking about how relieved his parents might be feeling right about now, knowing that their son had graduated, landed a job, and returned to the church.

And now it was Keith's turn: "So what brings you guys to Mosaic?"

"We're writing a book," said Casper.

"He's an atheist, and I'm a Christian," I said, adding my line as if on cue.

"We're visiting churches and writing about how we can have the same experience and come to different conclusions," said Casper, bringing our now familiar—at least to us—explanation in for a landing.

Then came the moment Casper and I had come to anticipate most as we watched the eyes of our new church friends to see how they would respond to our unusual job description.

Casper has told me that this moment, which happened just about every time we engaged someone, always made him feel different, but not in a good or a bad way. "Just different, like I've thrown my cards on the table, and where they were expecting maybe a pair, I've thrown four jacks. It's always such a major pronouncement, and I had no idea it would be like that. It's like the masks are off. No! Wait! I know what it is! It's like we're a bunch of guys talking guy talk, and suddenly I reveal the fact that I'm actually a woman disguised as a man. It's that kind of 'otherness.'"

I know what he means. After the announcement of our project, there is always a "gee-whiz" moment, but so far, that has always been followed by some of the most interesting conversations we have had, and this time was no exception. Keith was immediately (and genuinely) interested, and he corralled a guy walking through the lobby. "Hey, Erwin, you've got to meet these guys."

Erwin McManus himself just happened to be walking by. I couldn't have arranged this meeting if I had tried, and I almost shouted, "Thank you, Jesus," but I didn't want to alarm Casper the Friendly Atheist, or let Erwin the Emerging/Baptist/Famous Speaker think he had a wild Pentecostal on his hands, so I refrained.

"Where are you guys from?" Erwin asked.

"Seattle and San Diego," I said, nodding toward Casper. We quickly made "our pronouncement," as Casper would say, and got Erwin up to speed. The band continued to create the warm-up buzz in the main room, but I pulled my attention back to McManus and Casper in the lobby. This was not to be missed.

"Well, you'll be in the majority here," McManus told Casper confidently. "There are a lot of atheists in this church."

Casper looked to me as if to say, *Really?*

"One thing I noticed," said Casper, "is that most of the people here are pretty young—average age maybe nineteen?"

Erwin told us that his church doesn't attract young people so much as it does "the entrepreneurs, the creatives."

"Oh. It looks like young people to me."

Later Casper told me that "during that spiel, Erwin might as well have said, 'We're looking for people with iPods.'"

One thing I like about Casper and atheists in general is that due to their lack of reverence for our religion, they often see through things much more quickly than most Christians, and they feel free to tell me so.

Erwin then explained to us that Casper "may not understand" much of what he would see in church that day since Casper sees things from an atheist's perspective.

Casper said, "Well, I don't really consider atheism a perspective so much as a nonperspective—it's a nonperspective, a nonbelief. I mean, I can't invite you to an atheist meeting because we don't meet. . . . How do you rally around a nonbelief?"

Erwin disagreed, saying that atheism is like any belief system—Hinduism, Buddhism, etc.

"But all those still have belief in a supernatural God or deity of some sort, don't they?" asked Casper. "With atheism, there is no such thing."

Erwin said again that Casper was seeing things through an atheistic perspective and, therefore, did not understand.

"Well, yeah, from an atheistic perspective is how I see things," said Casper.

Erwin noticed that it was almost time to get onstage and parted company with us by saying, "Today we're featuring a film, and you're really going to love it. It was done by some guys from our church, and . . ." Erwin turned to Keith, who hadn't left our side, "I think it got an Oscar nomination for best foreign film."

I thought about how funny it is that here in L.A.—even in church—people name-drop with such sincerity. I wondered what Casper was thinking of Erwin McManus, but I didn't have time to ask. The service was about to begin. "C'mon, Casper. Let's go to church."

We finally made our way into the dimly lit and very funky (in a good way) auditorium to find a little table in the back, where we lit up our laptops and began to work. The room seated about five hundred people and had three large screens for PowerPoint.

These screens were different, though; they were round and looked like something out of the sixties—the psychedelic vibe again.

We had just a few minutes before the music really got started.

"So, tell me what you thought of McManus up close."

"Well, he was certainly direct. He looked right at me the entire time we spoke. He had an answer, immediately, for my every question. He was genuinely interested in our mission—our objective, I mean. Even if he kinda put me off by saying I wouldn't understand much of what I saw today since I see things from an atheist's perspective.

"And so far as the congregation is concerned—hundreds of atheists in his church? Did he say that to put me at ease, or to put me in my place?"

"I was wondering what that was about, too, Cas."

"It felt strange, but it made a little more sense when I saw that he thought atheism was a belief system on par with Buddhism. I got the feeling that for him, atheist means simply 'non-Christian,' not 'nonbelief.'

"All that aside, I certainly can see why he's a rock star in the Christian community. I mean, I couldn't tell if he was twenty-eight or fifty-eight. Every hair looked in place, and not a gray one among them. And he had a savvy way of talking to me; he didn't really fully answer my questions, yet I felt the conversation was progressing. It was weird, kind of like a salesman."

I agreed with Casper that it had seemed as if Erwin had not been listening so much as he had been trying to control the conversation.

Casper asked why he would do that: "Isn't the point to listen so that you can form relationships?"

"Yes, Casper, that's the point, but unfortunately I think we all, on some level, have a need to protect ourselves from authentic relationships."

I had seen that over and over during my career, especially among the pastors of larger churches. Sometimes it seems as if the same gift that enables people to become professional orators (a.k.a. pastors/ teachers) often disables them from connecting on a personal level.

I was so grateful for all the time I had recently spent with atheists. In doing so, I had learned that the best way to talk with them was to ask them what they really thought, rather than telling them what *I* thought they thought. I could tell Erwin had not been through atheist training in quite some time and could use a serious refresher course in listening.

"I get that need to protect yourself in the workplace, in the supermarket, in the street, but we're at church, aren't we?" asked Casper. "I would assume that those rules don't apply when you're talking about God. This should be a place where those worldly concerns, egos, and ulterior motives are left at the door, literally and figuratively. You and I always have—what appears to me anyway—real conversations."

"I'm all about keeping it real," I said.

I asked Casper what he thought thus far—having met the pastor and a few members of the congregation and seen the facility/ bar; did he think Mosaic was as different as so many in the Christian community think it is? Did he think Mosaic was different from other churches?

"Well, certainly having church in a bar is different. And this is clearly a church for young people. But do they stand for something different? Based on our discussions thus far, it seems to be pretty similar to other churches: Everyone must believe that Jesus is the

Son of God and died on the cross for our sins. So far as that goes, this is a church like any other.

"Band's good, though," Casper said, moving on to matters more immediate. "It's a real rock band: guitar, bass, drums, lead vocals. Maybe I'm only thinking that because we're at the kind of venue where I am accustomed to seeing real rock bands."

The band was stripped down, with a female lead singer and lighting that helped them look pretty cool as well. It felt more like a bar than a concert in that they were physically much closer to the audience, which was seated in something of a semicircle reaching back under the retro-theater balcony.

Casper and I were camped out under the balcony with our laptops balanced atop individual cocktail tables, the only light being provided compliments of Sony and Dell.

"How about the lyrics, the message, Casper?"

"Well, it's pretty much the same thing we've heard at some other stops: generic words of praise shared with us via PowerPoint. Although the words are a bit more accessible: 'Love is big, love is loud. We love you, Lord.' I get that. And, maybe because of the band's youth and energy and the intimacy of the venue, it seems more real to me compared to the arena vibe at the megachurches."

The music/worship experience "consisted of two rockers, one midtempo number, and a ballad," in the words of Casper the musician. Then the band bid us farewell with a "please be seated." Erwin took the stage, seating himself center stage on a stool.

At one point, he brought his teenage daughter onstage to make a point about the importance of their relationship, and it was clear that Erwin was very comfortable in front of his church. His voice has a theatrical sense to it, and the way he carries himself is measured, but warm in a public kind of way.

Over the course of about fifteen minutes, he told us:

"God seems like someone you can't really get to."

"God is a thinking God; God is a relational God."

"It's unthinkable that God would love you and me so much that he would make a sacrifice like that [Jesus' death]."

Following Erwin's sermon, we watched the movie he had told us about, but Casper and I had to leave before the closing comments were finished since we both had planes to catch. Just as they had promised, the parking volunteers made sure no one parked in front of Casper's Honda.

"Great service, Jim; these Mosaic guys pay attention to details."

On the way to the airport, I asked Casper what he thought about McManus's talk. Did he understand the language? Was there anything that inspired him?

"Sure, I understood it, but I thought it was pretty heavy—and pretty vague. Erwin told me in the lobby that I wouldn't understand a lot of what would go on there today—which, to be honest, is *not* a good way to keep a first-time visitor open-minded—but I did understand him when he said that God loves people.

"What I don't understand is why, and to what end? If God expresses his love for us by sacrificing his Son, how can that love possibly be returned? Is that sacrifice merely to be appreciated and recognized once, maybe twice a week, or must we do more? I would think more.

"And I think that's what I'm waiting for, Jim. After the sermon, and the music, and the bucket, I want to hear one answer to one simple question: What do you want me to do? I mean, we're talking about eternal salvation here, and if heaven *is* real, it can't be real easy getting in."

"Good point," I said. In the past, I might have pulled out the

Bridge tract at this point, but I knew we only had a few minutes to talk during our drive back to LAX, so I asked him what he thought about the offering.

"It was both laid back and insistent. First, I thought it might not be coming. After all, these are mostly kids here with little cash. But he did it with an unusual approach."

I wasn't sure what had been unusual about the offering at Mosaic. "What did you think was unusual about it?"

"Well, he said that for those of us just visiting today, we didn't have to give anything. Then he said that the congregation only gives because they love Jesus and this church. I wondered what that implies then about those of us who didn't give: We don't love Jesus? We don't like this church? Although it seemed so lackadaisical, I think it was actually one of the most aggressive solicitations yet."

Non-Christians can sometimes say the darndest things, I thought.

"And the movie that we watched was more food for thought, even if it was a tad short on calories."

The movie had been called *MOST*, but neither Casper nor I understood why. It was beautifully produced, it was nicely scripted, and it was wonderfully acted, but—and maybe this was because Erwin had given us a heads-up to look for biblical parallels—it did seem terribly predictable.

The movie had been about a train-switch operator faced with a terrible dilemma: In order to save a trainload of strangers, he must let his own son die.

I asked Casper if he saw the connection.

"Yes. That guy so loved the people on the train that he gave his only son—kind of impossible to miss."

Even Casper the atheist was able to easily make the connection with John 3:16. But then Casper surprised me.

"You know, as obvious as it was, it was also kind of moving. And I think I got a little bit of the message."

"What do you mean?"

"Well, the lives of the people on the train were not much different than our own—girl troubles, guy troubles, loneliness, selfishness, and so on. And many of the people weren't all that likeable. Yet the switch operator let his son die to save their lives. That moved me a little bit.

"Because sometimes I look at people and think, *If there's a God, why would he be interested in these jerks?* But I kind of see how that doesn't matter. It's not necessarily the sins of these people, or any people, that are in play."

At the end of the movie, McManus had spent a few minutes explaining it, and had even gone so far as to tell us why we should be moved by it.

"I didn't need his filter to tell me why or how to be moved," said Casper.

As we arrived at the airport, I thought about Casper's reaction. It certainly was not unique. Many of my young Christian friends also want the opportunity to come to their own, uncontrived conclusions. Maybe this is the heart of the matter when it comes to communicating with non-Christians. Rather than talking down to people we're trying to influence, we'd be wise to remember that just because they don't have God, it doesn't mean they have no soul.

MEGA IN THE MIDWEST
Willow Creek

We met up at O'Hare Airport, grabbed a rental car, and headed for Willow Creek Community Church, which is nestled securely in the upscale suburb of Barrington, about thirty miles outside of Chicago.

If you want to be famous, you have to be first. In that regard, Willow Creek has led the seeker-sensitive church growth movement for over twenty-five years. Just like Cher and Madonna, this church has become an only-one-name-needed sensation among pastors. Just say Willow and people know you mean The Church.

Willow hosts a national, multisite (via satellite TV) Leadership Summit every year for about seventy-five thousand leaders all over the world, and it is the founding church of the Willow Creek Association, a loose affiliation of congregations from a wide variety of denominations seeking to be like Willow.

I knew Casper had to meet the mega of the Midwest.

As big as Willow Creek is, we almost drove past it. There was no advance warning or roadside signage, just a big wall with big letters on the street: Willow Creek Community Church—which we saw in our rearview mirror.

"Hey, Jim . . . I think that was it."

Casper later asked why there were no billboards or signs pointing the way. I told him I thought it may be because of government regulations, but I wasn't sure.

"So, really, the only way you know it's there is if you're actively seeking it. Is that what they mean by seeker sensitive, Jim?"

We followed a long and winding road with color-coded signs, and parking areas A, B, C, D, E, and F from which to choose. It was kind of like a rural college campus. Various buildings sat off the road here and there, and lots and lots and lots of lots for parking. We chose to park next to the biggest building we could see, as we figured that's where we wanted to be.

It was Saturday night and time for some church, mega-style. Smiling people in matching shirts greeted us as we walked in; a visitor's center—Guest Central—was clear and easy to find. Casper ventured off to find a place where we could charge up our laptops.

"Over here, Jim. A guy said this place would be cool, though I refrained from telling him exactly why we needed it: 'Excuse me, could you help me find some Christian electricity for my atheistic computer?'"

From the lobby, we could see a waterfall, water fountains, escalators, thirty-foot-high ceilings, a bookstore, a restaurant, *and* a coffee shop.

"Hey, Jim, check it out: The restaurant has a salad bar, a grille—with an *e* mind you—a stir-fry station, a Mexican food counter, and a pizza counter. That's *five* choices for food, not including dessert!

"I feel like I'm in a Christian Nordstrom's. The colors are monochromatic, the lighting muted, and the chairs incredibly comfortable. I feel like I'm at a trade show or something. What's with all the people wearing official-looking name badges? How many people come here, anyway?"

I could see that Casper had a lot of questions and opinions already, and we hadn't even been inside the stadium—I mean, sanctuary—yet.

I told Casper that more than twenty thousand people attend this church and its affiliate campuses every weekend. And that there are so many kids coming and going for Sunday school that they have to use a fingerprint scanner to keep track of them and their parents.

"A fingerprint scanner? Holy smokes! How do they manage this operation?"

"Is that what it feels like to you, Casper? An operation?"

"Yeah," he said as we walked into the sanctuary. "I mean, just the infrastructure investment alone! And—oh my God—look at this place!"

It was the first time I'd heard Casper say God's name in this way, and I could see why. We had entered Willow's main stage theater, which can hold 7,500 people. It has two balconies, four huge projection screens, a soundproof area in the back for crying babies, a sign language section, and a separate handicapped section. Casper was clearly impressed, so it seemed a good time to ask him what he thought.

"The first thing that comes to mind is how much did this place cost to build? How much to keep it running? What are their electricity bills? And, maybe because of our 'mission,' the next thing I wonder is, is this what they think their God wants?"

"What do you mean?" I asked. "Do you think God would be unhappy to see so many people coming together in one place to worship? Do you think God doesn't want Christian churches like Willow to have a greater impact in the world?"

"Well, I don't have an answer for those questions. At least not the one you may need. . . ."

"But that's why I hired you, Casper—because you are willing to question everything we Christians hold sacred and tell us what you think, no holds barred."

The band then started playing. The call to worship was underway. So we started there: "What do you think about the band? On a scale of one to five . . ."

"Gotta go low here, Jim. The guy is wearing makeup, sweating like a Vegas Elvis, and singing secular songs [U2's "Beautiful Day," to be precise]. They get a one."

"But check out their chops! These folks can really play."

"Yeah, Jim. But check out the people here. No one moving, a few people clapping in time—sort of. This stuff doesn't seem to be doing anything for anybody. And they played a U2 song! And now, listen to this song. Look at that singer's smiling face and listen to those lyrics: 'This world holds nothing for me.' How can you sing that and smile?"

"Okay, Casper, so the music isn't really doing it for you. What do you think of the congregation? All these people?"

"Look around. Nearly every person in this church is white. No big deal; we're in a relatively white part of the country, and we're in a church that has more in common with white culture than others. But look at the singers on the stage; look at the slide show playing behind the band. It's the United Colors of Benetton. Kind of strikes me the way some political conventions do: Sure, our leaders and policies are white-bread, but look at these black people here, too! It's presenting a false inclusiveness, I think."

Casper certainly had the details right. Everyone that we could see in the congregation was white, but there was certainly a seemingly intentional ethnic balance onstage.

As the music was coming to a close, Bill Hybels, the founding pastor, took the stage. I was pleased because I had heard that he had turned the church over to new leadership, and I wasn't expecting to see the man himself. But there he was doing the announcements and setting up the offering.

I was pretty impressed with the fact that Hybels had successfully (I assume, anyway) handed over the leadership of the church and yet was still able to handle what would typically be viewed as a low-level responsibility—and no one made a big deal of it by saying (drumroll), "Ladies and gentlemen! Please welcome to the stage none other than Bill Hybels!"

Casper commented that "they break out the big guns to get the plate passed," but then he said something that surprised me: "But I actually like what Hybels said."

"What? I thought you said he was just the big gun?"

"Yeah, but he made first-timers feel okay about not kicking in when he said, 'Visitors, just let the plate go by.' I think that's important: You don't ask someone to pay for your services sight unseen. It makes sense from a marketing point of view as well. It's like today is a risk-free trial—pay nothing now!

"And that simple difference, the leader of this church saying, 'Just let the plate go by,' no strings attached, well, that set me at ease. Maybe it's because as a kid going to church there was always a sense that if you're not kicking in, you're not doing your part . . . and you'd get guilty looks from the other folks in the pew, of course. And I almost felt at ease at Mosaic, but then there was the little twist, the little whiff of guilt at the end: 'We only give because we love God.' But maybe Erwin needs the money more."

Then Hybels basically read the announcements and talked about what was going on at Willow. "Three hundred people will be baptized tomorrow," he said excitedly.

Casper was astounded: "How does that work? I mean, logistically? Is there a big line going down to the lake? Do they use a Super Soaker? Will it be a flume ride like at Disneyland?"

"It's the first one: a line down to the lake."

But I could see that, although he was joking, Casper didn't think a flume ride would be entirely out of the question here at

Willow Creek. At least not for a church with the resources this one has.

Then Hybels mentioned that prayers were answered because he had landed a meeting with Bono and had just flown over to Ireland to shoot a video interview with him.

"I'm sorry, Jim. Did I just hear him say that he landed an interview with Bono because people were praying for it?"

"Yeah. Why is that unusual?"

"Well, it seems like a gaudy use of the power of prayer. An interview with Bono? Is that the kind of thing that people at Willow pray for? Why stop there? Why not pray for a worldwide tour opening for U2? Why not pray that Bill Hybels becomes U2's bass player?"

I laughed out loud, trying to envision this possibility, although I imagined Hybels could probably carry his own with the gig.

"I mean, come on. People are being killed needlessly in every corner of the world, kids are starving, and people are praying for their pastor to meet a rock star? That's ludicrous."

Other atheists had asked me about this casual view of prayer Christians seem to hold. I knew that nothing I could say would convince Casper that somehow it isn't a waste of time for Christians to pray for parking spots or interviews with famous rock stars when people are starving in Rwanda. But his questions stuck in my mind nonetheless, and it felt almost as if God was asking me these same questions as well—through Casper of all people!

Gene Appel, the new lead pastor at Willow, took the mike and introduced Derek and Greg, two guys whose lives had been changed by being baptized at Willow.

Derek was raised Catholic (he even referred to his baptism as a "Mass"), and his story was one we have heard before: a lot of church when he was young, less as he got older and went to college (which Appel said was "when many people drift away from Christ"), some drug use, and finally, the need to get his life back on track. We then saw a video of him being baptized in a big Plexiglas tank on the very stage where he was speaking.

Greg's story was a little more interesting: He was a seventh-degree black belt, a former bodyguard to entertainers, and a mercenary soldier who, among other things, had killed people overseas. He was in spiritual pain over the life he was living when his brother—a "Creeker"—suggested he come to a service.

But Greg was reticent: "Can God really forgive someone like me?" Pastor Appel appeared deeply moved, his voice breaking as he described the day Greg was baptized, which we also saw replayed on the big screen.

"What did you think of that?" I asked Casper.

"Well, I'd rather have Greg saved and here at Willow Creek than murdering people for money in other countries."

Casper has a way of putting things that typically does away with any kind of euphemism.

"And it was moving to see how much his story affected the pastor as well. I also get why Derek and Greg both needed not only to be baptized, but also to tell their stories. But especially Greg. It's good Derek went first, because Greg's story is pretty tough to follow."

Then Pastor Appel urged anyone who had not been baptized to come tomorrow, his voice again breaking as he described the importance of being baptized. (Casper would later dismiss this voice breaking as "out of hand. . . . It felt real the first time, and then, the next few times, it became evident that it was only a tool, and not heartfelt emotion—pretty sneaky.")

Pastor Appel reminded us that many people at Willow "have yet to go public" by being baptized and that it was important because you never know "what happens five minutes after you die."

Casper dismissed this, too, and said, "That reminds me of what happened at Outreach."

"Outreach Marketing?" I asked.

"Yeah, Jim. When I moved to San Diego with my family, my first job was at Outreach Marketing. There's no big story about how that came into being. I needed a job; they had a job. But soon after I started working there, I knew it wasn't the place for me."

"You mean an atheist didn't fit in at the vortex of evangelical communication? I can't imagine!"

"Very funny. Yes, I'm an atheist for one, but two, the pay was lousy. So after about two months, I found a new job. On my last day at Outreach, the VP of marketing wanted to meet with me. I thought it was to go over proprietary information, etc. But he wanted to talk to me about my beliefs! I told him I was an atheist. He said, 'You don't believe that Jesus died for your sins?' I gave him the old one-two: 'No, I don't. And even more to the point, I don't believe there's a God at all.'

"He looked more than a little shocked. *How could this person we hired not even believe in God?* So he tried the same approach Appel just tried: 'Have you thought about what would happen if you were in a fatal car accident on your way home?'

"Now it was my turn to be shocked. Had the VP of marketing cut my brake lines or something? And I thought, *What a ridiculous question! A fatal car wreck? That's the best you've got?* But I told him, 'Well, fatal—I'd die. That's what would happen.'

"'But what about after that?' he asked. 'Well, I hope someone would clean up the mess,' I replied. And then I said, 'Listen. You believe in an omnipotent God, right? So you wouldn't be surprised to see people flying, or a two-hundred-foot-tall Jesus come walking out of the ocean. Whereas I would. Those things would surprise me very much.'

"And that was pretty much the end of our conversation. He threatened my life, I mocked his beliefs, see you later."

"So you saw this as a pretty ham-fisted and nonhuman way to approach you, Casper?"

"Right, and it's too bad that that lazy approach to saving souls is what I'm experiencing here at Willow."

"But you *are* going to die, Casper. So far the stats are pretty solid on that one. Are you saying you are unconcerned with what happens following your certain death—whether it be in a car wreck or quietly in your sleep?"

"*Et tu*, Jim? I don't know what happens following my death, your death, or anyone's death. I mean, are you holding out on me? In your conversations with God, have you been given any proof of what happens after we die?"

"No, Casper, all I have is faith—that's it—no proof. The fact is I can't prove one thing about what I believe to you. All I have is a hope, and the reality is neither of us will know who is right until we actually die."

Casper's mouth was agape, and he was silent for a bit. When he spoke again, it was much more quietly.

"Wow, Jim. I have never heard it put that way before. I've never heard anyone admit that it's all based on faith. So often people precede an attempt to get me to join up with Jesus with a threat and an unprovable claim: Choose Christ, because you're going to die. I always think, *That's it? That's the pitch?* I mean, what else is in the package?

"Look at the signs." I was tempted to look to the sky, but instead I looked to where Casper was pointing: large screens that said "Just Follow."

"What does that mean—just follow? Don't you have to put something on the line? I know that when people followed Jesus in first-century Palestine, they were risking life and limb. When people followed Martin Luther King Jr., they were risking arrest. When they followed Gandhi, they risked bodily harm and even death. But what does *just follow* mean here and in this context? Christianity can't be just getting baptized or just following. You have to put something on the line, I think."

"Well, Casper, *just follow* means give your whole life to Jesus; follow him, place your trust in his story and in his version of reality."

Casper asked me how I could follow someone who's not around, and I told him that Jesus *is* around—he's everywhere.

"I've heard that before," said Casper. "And I'm sure that Pastor Appel would say the exact same thing. So let me be more specific: If Jesus is everywhere, and everyone here is following him, what do you think this enlightened, impassioned, and above all, humble carpenter from Galilee would say about Plexiglas dunking tanks, millionaire pastors, camera cranes, and music coming straight outta Branson? Is this what Jesus had in mind for church?"

Pastor Gene Appel wrapped up the service by reminding us that the first step in obedience is baptism; this did little to pacify or edify my friend Casper. As we walked out of the service, Casper put it plainly once more: "Just follow. . . . following is a means, not an end. Do all these people doing the following have any idea where they're going or what they'll do when they get there?"

I told Casper that Willow has actually created tons of opportunities for people to serve others and participate in making the world a better place.

"Why didn't they include something about that today, Jim?"

"I guess there just wasn't enough time today."

"Maybe they'll read our book, Jim, and see that—for people outside their church anyway—talking about the deeds they do beats vague platitudes like *just follow* every time."

Defending the Space

From Talking to Listening

In my first book, *Evangelism Without Additives*, I talk about *free attention giveaways.* This involves simple practices like asking someone, "How are you?" and actually listening. We've been experimenting for a number of years to see what happens when, rather than asking people to give us their time and attention, we offer them ours.

For some reason, Christians continue to believe that we can talk people into following Jesus. That's why we think we need to memorize the right words or even our own story (as if we can't remember our own story). We all know the impact it has on us when someone listens to us. This simple act is so rare that whoever practices it (even poorly) is immediately set apart in our minds as someone we would like to spend more time with.

Defending the space means we practice listening.

HELEN, THE ALMOST-AN-ATHEIST, TAKES US TO CHURCH

First Presbyterian

Helen is what you'd call *almost* an atheist.

Helen used to be a Christian; she knows the Bible intimately because she's been studying and teaching it for almost twenty years. The whole religion thing finally got to her and, slowly but surely, she stopped believing in Christianity and quit church.

She soon began to think of herself as an atheist—a shocking fact she had barely told any of her Christian friends and acquaintances. It was around this time that our blog caught her attention.

Following Off The Map's winning bid for the eBay atheist, our eBay Atheist blog became an online watercooler of sorts where Christians and atheists could dialogue about their differences. (And that blog, not so coincidentally, was the launchpad for the book you now hold in your hands.)

We intentionally used the word *dialogue* instead of *debate* because we knew our visitors could find a debate anywhere. But a good dialogue—where people would listen and respond, as opposed to just arguing their point or perspective—was much more difficult to come by. Helen was one of the first people to check out the blog.

At first—and as is the style on most blogs and online forums— she did not use her real name, so we only knew her as "Ir." We didn't even know if she was a man or woman. (Many bloggers assumed she was male, which amused her greatly!)

Helen/Ir was impressed from the start that we were hosting a respectful learning group between atheists and Christians. She later told me, "I had been participating in online discussions between Christians and atheists for five years, and I had never seen Christians and atheists 'listening' to each other so well!"

She was very pleased that Off The Map wasn't using the blog to set up or trick people into becoming Christians. She was delighted to see Christians *asking* atheists what they thought and—*gasp*—even agreeing with them from time to time. Consequently, Helen got stuck in the Off The Map cul-de-sac and, along with many others, started dialoguing.

We noticed that Helen was able to avoid arguments, ask thoughtful questions, and affirm people from either side of the issue with generosity and authenticity. She soon became the real leader of the blog, and we eventually turned the keys to the technology over to her so that she could design and lead more online conversations.

Now we have several blogs. Helen oversees them all and leads the discussion on Conversation at the Edge (http://www.conversationattheedge.com) a conversation for people with and without belief systems.

Once she was a regular part of our eBay atheist blog community, Helen and I began talking online more and more. I told her that I was not threatened by her rejection of Christianity. She could share anything with me—in fact, I hoped she would. I was curious to hear her story, especially since it was turning out to have a lot in common with mine. Among other things, she said, "Wow, Jim—you really get it, don't you? I never thought I'd find a follower of Jesus who understood why I quit church!"

We met for coffee one weekend when I was in Chicago. Helen

has lived there for several years with her husband and children, although she was born and raised in England. There was a question I had to ask. "Helen, are you *really* an atheist?"

She thought for a moment. "I don't know, Jim. I really thought I was a few months ago. I knew I wasn't a Christian. But Off The Map has helped me understand that I don't have to be a Christian to be a follower of Jesus. Maybe I am still a follower after all!"

Since Casper and I were going to be in Chicago visiting churches, I asked Helen to find a midsize church for us to attend. We had been on the megachurch tour and needed to check in with churches that are closer in size to those the majority of American Christians attend.

Before church started, Casper, Helen, and I grabbed a cup of coffee. Helen and Casper had already met online via the blog, but over coffee, they got to know each other a bit better.

While those around us spent this early part of Sunday morning either reading the newspaper or making small talk about sports and what was on TV last night, we passed an hour or so good-naturedly sparring on subjects like the origins of our people, planet, and cosmos. Then, after much good talk and coffee, we went to church. Helen decided to take us to First Presbyterian Church of River Forest (an upper-middle-class neighborhood not far from downtown Chicago). This was Helen's first time visiting a service there, too, although she was expecting to see some Christians that she knew from the neighborhood. When we walked past the choir on our way in, a choir member recognized her and said hello.

We found an open pew and sat down, Helen on one side of me and Casper on the other. Casper and I immediately opened up our laptops. I had warned Helen about this a few days earlier:

"Helen, you're going to be okay with us taking notes throughout the service, right?"

"Of course!" she'd responded. "So long as you don't mind me participating in the worship—even though I'm almost an atheist!"

And writing about church was nothing new to Helen anyway. She had just sent an article—"Why I Don't Go to Church Anymore"—to a local newspaper.

"Hey, I'm glad my newspaper article hasn't run yet—it makes being here today less complicated," she commented.

"You were brave to write that, Helen. Remember how afraid you were that someone you knew might read your comments when you first posted on our blog? And that people would find out that you weren't the Christian they thought you were? You've come a long way in the last few months."

Helen was curious about the notes I was taking. From time to time she looked at my screen to read what I had written, and smiled. I knew what she was thinking. When we had coffee together, I'd told Helen about my plan to start a new blog where churchgoers as well as outsiders could post "brutally honest" reviews of church services. Helen *loved* the idea, and with her help we launched Church Rater. As the service was beginning, Helen pointed out the elaborate floral display in front of the pulpit. "Look at that—someone must have just gotten married—or died."

Casper and I thought that was pretty funny—yesterday's funeral flowers were today's sermon flowers. However, the minister soon made an announcement about how the flowers were given in appreciation for the Williams family, who were moving to the West Coast. The church wanted to thank them for their contribution to the contemporary worship ministry.

"I guess they aren't recycled flowers after all!" Helen said.

This is the kind of church I would never have been able to fit into as a young believer. The wood paneling, formal hymns, well-performed piano duets, and old money made it feel more like an English hunting lodge than a church to me. I wondered if Casper was having similar kinds of thoughts.

I didn't have to wait long to find out. It was time to sing, and to my surprise, Casper reached for his hymnal like a teenager reaching for a PlayStation. He stood up and began singing—loud and proud. I thought that perhaps Casper liked the hymns so much because he's such a good singer—as anyone who has seen his band perform will surely attest to. (Yes, that was a blatant commercial for his band.)

When the hymn was over, Casper sat down with a smile. "Ahhhh . . . feels like home, Jim!"

I was mystified. "What do you mean, Casper?"

There was no time for an explanation—we would have to take this up later. The pastor had stepped forward and was about to speak to the congregation.

Unlike Erwin McManus or Bill Hybels, this pastor was decidedly unhip. Pastor David Worth is probably in his late fifties and looked very much like an executive. He was just back from an important Presbyterian conference, and he was reporting to the congregation on decisions the pastors had made about the seventh commandment and other Presbyterian insider matters.

"The church is founded on Christ," he began. (Casper later asked, "Was there ever any question?")

"From now on, all baptisms will be done in the name of the Father, the Son, *and* the Holy Ghost." (Casper found this a little baffling, too: "What were they baptizing folks under before if not the big three?")

In spite of all her knowledge of church and the Bible, Helen was confused too. She had her pew Bible open and was counting the commandments, trying to figure out which one was number seven. "Why didn't he tell us which one is the seventh commandment?"

After finishing his report from the conference, the pastor asked the deacon and elders who had just been elected to come forward.

Helen listened as the new leaders pledged their allegiance to God, the church, and the congregation. "How can they possibly keep all these promises?" she asked.

She told me that it reminded her of the promises she had made to various churches over the years. At the time she thought nothing of it. Now she was wondering why she had so unquestioningly given virtual strangers such authority over her.

Another hymn followed (Casper was happy). Presbyterians seem to favor quality over quantity—a lot of very important and hard-to-understand words rather than the standard "Jesus, I praise you" fifty times in a row that we had grown accustomed to in our megachurch experiences.

Then it was time for the pastor to read a prayer of confession.

"We confess that we have been concerned with ordinary things and forgotten the global things. . . . Your reign is magnificent, but you want to use even the ordinary. . . . Lord God, help us get back to your global purpose. . . . We pray these things in your heavenly holy name. . . ."

This was *very* serious stuff, and it helped me remember why I was initially attracted to Pentecostalism. He ended the prayer with this old English declaration: "Be ye glad."

"'Ye'? That's language that keeps the church contemporary?" Casper whispered.

As the sermon neared its end, Casper and I waited for the moment we had come to expect at the close of every church service. We call it "the breaking-voice phenomenon."

For some reason, in virtually every church, the pastor ends the service sounding as if he's about to cry. Christians are largely inured to this. It's so common that we either endure it or enjoy it because it's the tribal signal that services are almost done.

But not at First Pres. Here, Pastor Worth added his own twist by simply lowering his voice to almost a whisper. Casper and I later called it "the quiet voice phenomenon."

Helen noticed it too. She moved close enough so I could hear her and said, "I don't get it. There's been nothing that offended me about this service, and I like how they aren't putting on a show to entertain me. What's going on here feels real and authentic. Yet instead of appreciating it, I just feel . . . *bored*. I could never come here week after week. I'm barely making it through this one service!"

I wasn't especially surprised to hear this since I felt so disengaged myself. But the real conundrum wasn't Helen's response to the service, or mine; it was Casper's. Helen was bored, I was disengaged, yet Casper was, well, *giddy*.

"Casper, I think that of the three of us, you, the *atheist*, enjoyed this service most!" said Helen.

I jumped in too: "Yeah, Cas. Explain why you felt so at home here. I thought you would like a church like this the least, being of pure atheist stock. Isn't your dad a lifetime atheist?"

"Well, yes and no, Jim. He's only been an atheist for *my life-time*. It was at my baptism—yes, I was baptized Catholic; it was the style at the time—that he started to seriously consider atheism."

"Wait, Casper, you're telling me that it was a baptismal service, a ritual we Christians hold extremely dear, that started your dad down the path to atheism?"

"Pretty much, Jim. It was 1968, and the Catholic church my dad's family belonged to had just stopped doing baptisms in Latin. So my dad got to hear the words loud and clear. And when he saw this innocent little baby and heard the priest talking about casting sin out of this beautiful, harmless creature, he just couldn't see the sense in it."

But I still was not entirely sure what gave Casper that feeling of home, sweet home, at First Pres.

"So did your dad then move from Catholicism to Presbyterianism? You said this church feels like home."

"No, my dad avoided church for as long as I can remember. This feels like home because I went to a church just like this when I was around seven or eight years old: First Presbyterian in Hartford, Connecticut. My mom sang in churches as a soloist—a hired gun, I believe.

"She was working at First Presbyterian in Hartford, and being the relatively religious person she was, whenever she went to church, she made sure her kids went too.

"You know what's weird, Jim, is that I never before thought about whether or not she got paid for singing. But now that I've been visiting all these churches and seeing the caliber of musicians in many of them, I'm wondering if there's a cottage industry of musicians who get hired to play in churches? The ones here at First Presbyterian [River Forest] looked like they were definitely part of the congregation, but the ones at, say, Willow Creek, seemed like seasoned professionals. So are they hired guns or not, Jim?"

"Well," I answered, "like you said earlier, yes and no. In some cases they're paid, and in others, not. But generally, churches would at least require that you be a Christian to play Christian music—I guess."

As I was talking, it occurred to me: *Who makes up these rules anyway?* No wonder it's confusing to non-Christians who are trying to figure out who's in and who's out in our churches.

It seemed to me that Casper's happy memories were mostly responsible for him enjoying the service. I was curious to see whether he agreed.

"Casper, was it the actual church service that moved you? Or was it the idea of it, the memories, the nostalgia?"

"Tough to say. My memory is certainly having an effect on my experience right now. I mean, I even got confirmed in a church like this. I said the oath, took Communion. Obviously, I wasn't too sure what it was about, but it seemed like the right thing to do at the time. Probably for the same reason getting me baptized may have seemed like the thing for my parents to do."

"Right," I responded. "There are a lot of those kinds of decisions and rituals that make up the fabric of what has come to be called Christianity in our country. It's sometimes difficult to separate what's Christian from what's simply American."

We had another service to attend that morning, so we packed up our laptops and prepared to leave. Many in the congregation were still standing in small groups around the church, talking with each other. Casper commented, "This is neat—in the megachurches everyone seemed so eager to rush off!"

Helen wasn't so impressed. "Casper, it's nice that they're talking to each other, but how come no one has come over to greet you and Jim? Aren't they at least curious about why two guys were here typing on laptops? Surely they noticed!"

I told Helen that in all our church visits, hardly anyone had voluntarily spoken to us. This was the norm, not the exception.

We walked back to our cars. After saying good-bye to Helen (our almost-an-atheist colleague), Casper (my I-know-I'm-currently-an-atheist coauthor) and I headed out the door into Chicagoland.

In the car, Casper and I discussed Helen's observation. In fact, not only had no one spoken to us at the end, not one person voluntarily spoke to us the whole time we were inside their building.

I told Casper that I'd love to start a new seminar, one that will help churches realize that one very simple action on their part could make a very big difference in how people perceive them.

"You mean the 'just say hi' idea?"

"Right," I said. "In fact I think I'll call it the 'Just Say Hi Church Growth Seminar.' Here's my idea. We tell pastors to retire all of their ushers."

"I bet a lot of those people would be relieved to not *have* to be nice every Sunday, Jim, but who would take the place of all those unusually friendly people we've encountered at the front door of every church we've attended so far?"

"That's where the 'just say hi' part comes in, Cas. We tell pastors to find five to ten people who are willing to do one simple thing every time they come to church."

"What's that, Jim?"

"Just say hi, Casper. That's it. They would agree to say hi to three people who are new to them, and then they would be done for the day."

"Sounds kind of canned, Jim. What's the difference between ushers at the door and roaming greeters?"

"Simply perception," I said. "Think about how impressed we are when anyone makes the smallest gesture toward us voluntarily."

"I see where you're coming from, Jim. When we were approached by Randi at Saddleback, or Keith at Mosaic, it definitely made an impression. And I'm a seasoned atheist. Imagine if I were what you call a seeker! I would be very impressed if someone did something even as small as saying hi to me. It seems small and very doable. I wonder why people need a seminar to remind them of that?"

"Good question," I said. "So other than no one speaking to us, were there any other thoughts you had or any you're having now?"

"Well, right now I'm having one thought, and it is most certainly based on nostalgia and not the sermon. I want to go to Burger King. Every Sunday, my mother would swing us by Burger King on the way home, and I want to complete the experience."

"Okay, but beyond Burger King and memory lane, what did you think of the service? Of the congregation? Are you able to offer an honest report sans nostalgia?"

"I'd like to say yes, but it may be tough. That church was *so* much like the one I went to when I was young, *everything* resonated with me. Even the prayers. I noticed that after the prayer was said, there was a moment—a long moment—of silence. I wondered if at that moment everyone was echoing what they heard in the prayer or saying their own prayers . . . but when I looked at the kids in the church at that moment, I had a pretty good idea what was on their minds."

"What's that?"

"When's this gonna be over so we can go to Burger King?"

"So was that it, Casper? Just a trip down memory lane?"

"No, I put my atheist observer hat on, too. One thing I really liked was their use of the Bible. In many of the churches we've 'worked,' they pull one sentence or even just one clause from one verse, and we get no context.

"I often feel like the pastor makes up his mind on what he wants to say and then does a keyword search in the Bible to find whatever verse he can to support it. But here, we read a whole passage (Acts 26:1-29), and we got the whole story in context. And yeah, while there was more than a fair share of *thees* and *thous*, I really enjoyed it.

"The Bible is chock-full of interesting stories, and sometimes it may be more effective just to let them speak for themselves."

Casper the Friendly Atheist. Telling me—a pastor with thirty years of experience reading, decoding, interpreting, relaying, and rehashing the Bible—what it's all about. I was just about to respond to him when we were interrupted by a disembodied voice, coming to us from out of the air: *Welcome to Burger King. May I take your order?*

BIG CHURCH OR CHURCH BIG
Lawndale

As I mentioned in the introduction to this book, Christians often use the word *lost* to describe non-Christians. Christians have *found* Jesus, but everyone else is *lost*. In my book *Evangelism Without Additives* (formerly titled *a.k.a. "Lost"*), I describe in more detail why I don't like this term or subscribe to this view.

But still, as we drove toward Lawndale Community Church in Chicago, I couldn't resist the temptation to use that word to tell Casper what I thought.

"Face it, Casper: You really are lost."

"Yeah, no kidding, Jim. Let me see those directions again."

Fresh off our visit to First Presbyterian in River Forest, we were now headed into Chicago's inner city, hoping to make it in time for the 11:00 service at Lawndale. But as of 10:45 a.m., there was no church in sight.

First Presbyterian and Lawndale Community Church are a mere ten-minute drive from each other, but as we'd soon see, the cultural distance between them is immeasurable.

As a Christian, I've often wondered how churches can use the same words, claim the same beliefs, and declare themselves to be totally committed to Christ and yet be so different in the values they present and the practices they undertake.

If, as we like to say, we're all serving the same God, one would think we would all be on the same page about the things that matter most. One (maybe an atheist named Casper?) might also think that all Christians share the same values and maintain the same practices regardless of socioeconomic standing or cultural biases.

What if following Jesus meant something simple and easily definable and defendable to an outsider—like providing affordable housing to people all over the globe? What if that's all we did? Would that be so bad? At least then everyone would know what Christians did and what was expected of someone who joined them.

Or what if we were known as the people who adopted all the unwanted babies . . . or what if Christians were thought of as being the best listeners in the world? (We aren't.) Why are there such glaring discrepancies among churches regarding what it means to be a follower of Christ?

Case in point right here in Chicago: How is it possible that two churches so close to each other geographically and in their professed beliefs can be so dramatically different (as we would soon see)? Is it all cultural? Is that okay?

Okay. I'm off my soapbox.

I had specifically planned this sequence of visits to provide us with some serious contrast. But it looked like we might be missing out on church number two. Then Casper said, "There's Lawndale! Oh . . . forget it; it's a dental clinic or something."

I smiled and told Casper we were here. We were standing about two hundred feet from the front door, but Casper couldn't see it. Cars whisked by as he scanned up and down the busy street in front of the church.

"Is that it over there?" He was pointing toward a three-story brick–and–glass structure that appeared to be the newest building in the neighborhood.

That building sure looked a lot like some of the megachurches we'd visited—modern, clean, multistoried—but then Casper read the sign.

"Lawndale Health Center. All right, so we're in the right neighborhood at least."

"Actually, Cas, that's part of the church, or better yet, evidence that the church has been here. Lawndale Community Church started a free medical clinic on this street a number of years ago, and it grew until it was eventually turned over to another nonprofit that focused solely on providing low-cost or free medical services to the underserved of Lawndale."

"Well done! Now *that's* what I'm talking about! If you're going to be a 'community' church, serve your community. So where's the big building itself?"

"Where's what, Casper?"

"The *church* Jim, Lawndale Community Church—you know, where people meet, sing, clap, pray, and preach?"

"Keep looking," I told him.

I was enjoying the try-to-find-the-church game.

"Is that it?"

"No, that's Hope House, a recovery place for drug addicts."

"Okay, here's my final guess, Jim. That big red sign down on the corner, is that it?"

"No, Cas. That's the pizza restaurant Lawndale started with a local chain in Chicago to provide a place where families could eat together. But more important, the restaurant also enables them to provide jobs for people in their recovery programs, to help these people get back into the workforce."

"Wow. So is that it, Jim? Is this like a nonchurch church? All good deeds in the community and no preaching, praying, singing?"

Suddenly the Lawndale nine o'clockers began to emerge from the inconspicuous front door of Lawndale Community Church.

"All right, strike that. I see a church. Let's go." We made our way across the street, dodging traffic as we went.

I figure that what we experienced must be what the average person does too. Stand on the street in front of Lawndale Community Church, and you'll see what church growth *backward* looks like.

Instead of growing a *Big Church* (the Three *B*s) Lawndale has grown a *Church Big*. They have provided practical services for people who need them, and they've been working hard within an existing community that could use the help. Lawndale is what many today are calling a missional church.

Pastor Wayne Gordon, Lawndale's founder and leader, moved from the suburbs to the inner city thirty years ago to start this church—or more accurately, to extend a movement: the Christian Community Development Association (CCDA).

The CCDA is a group of Christians led by John Perkins who practice not the Three *B*s but what they call the Three *R*s: relocation, reconciliation, and redistribution.

I shouted to Pastor Gordon as he walked by: "Hey, Coach!"

He's a former wrestling coach who prefers to be called Coach rather than Pastor, and I wanted to introduce him to Casper. I had met Coach a couple of years earlier at a class I was taking at his church. He nodded to us and said a quick hello, but he had to get to the business at hand.

"Jim, he's a white guy, and this is a mostly black church. What's up with that? Did he take this church over from someone else?"

"Nope. This is his church, always has been. In case you couldn't tell, Casper, Coach Gordon has a different way of doing church than a lot of what we've seen so far."

In his book *Real Hope in Chicago*, Gordon put it this way:

"I realized that 'get saved' evangelism was designed for suburban folk. It had little meaning in an urban context. . . . People in the city are not encumbered primarily with feelings of guilt. Their deepest feelings are of hopelessness."*

For almost thirty years, Lawndale and its people have consistently disciplined themselves around the mission of bringing the Kingdom of God to their neighborhood in very practical ways. And they call people to follow Jesus by faith as well.

"Lawndale started small," I told Casper. "Their first act of serving was to provide a washer and dryer for the community. Then they moved on to larger projects (a day-care center) and to still larger projects (a medical clinic). Today, Lawndale has its own development corporation, which builds homes for people in and out of the community and essentially deletes any builder's profit off of the final sales price, thus providing instant equity and economic power for people who have never owned a home.

"This isn't just a group of people trying to be nice, or talking about doing good, or even simply doing good works to earn a spot in heaven. The people of Lawndale seem to really believe that when they build a home for a low-income person in an abandoned neighborhood—or when they build a health clinic or a day-care center or a school—they are obeying what Jesus told us to do: Bring the Kingdom of God to Earth."

I was showing my bias, but Casper was a tough critic and could be trusted to ignore me if my description didn't match his experience.

"While Lawndale's current attendance averages a respectable five hundred, their budget matches a church of five thousand and

---

*Wayne L. Gordon and Randall Frame, *Real Hope in Chicago* (Grand Rapids: Zondervan, 1995), 170.

reveals another story that can't be measured by worship attendance," I said. "They get much of their income from the same sources other nonprofits do: grants, subsidized loans, and sales of the properties they develop. And all the money gets plowed back into the Lawndale Development Corporation."

"Sounds great, Jim; let's see if they preach what they practice."

I told Casper that that was a nice twist on a very old saying, and we made our way through the packed foyer into the sanctuary. It would be more accurate to call it a warehouse instead of a sanctuary. It was a loftlike space with brick walls, a wooden ceiling, and folding chairs fanning out from a small wooden platform in the middle of the room. No traditional altar, no camera cranes, no fog machines, no waterfalls (plenty of water stains, however), and lots and lots of people filling in the rows of chairs.

The congregation was mostly made up of black people, but there was a handful of white people, too. I couldn't help but think about where Casper and I were just two hours ago. And I again thought how good it would be if pastors encouraged people to visit other churches once a month. Not only do Christians need to see how other Christians worship, we also need to know what it feels like to be an outsider. As Casper was showing me, outsiders tend to be *much* more objective. This kind of exercise could probably even help Christians better understand their own beliefs.

"Check it out, Jim." Casper directed my attention to the projector screen where the phrase "Never, Never, Never Give Up!" was illuminated.

"It's a lot like Saddleback, where the message was 'Don't Give Up.' But I gotta tell you, it makes a lot more sense here, in this neighborhood, and with that much emphasis, too: never, never, *never*."

Then the music kicked in. There was a band—keyboards, bass,

drums, guitar—and a group of about six singers standing on the platform in the center of the room, singing and grooving to the music.

No clear worship leader, no separation between the audience and the performers, no one's face projected onto a ten-by-twenty-foot screen—just music. And it was working wonders. People were dancing, clapping, singing along, shouting out "Amen."

"Bass player's awesome." Casper was enjoying himself once more.

"What about the PowerPoint, Cas? It bothered you at the other churches. Does it bother you here?"

"Churches using technology to communicate better doesn't bother me at all," he said. "What was bothering me at those churches was the amount of money that was clearly being spent on technology and equipment, which I see as vain at best, hypocritical at worst. How are you helping others by spending your offering money on a Hollywood stage show?

"But more than that, it's the *massive* disconnect between the words on the PowerPoint projection and the stuff I saw in the church. That woman at Willow smiling as she sang, 'This world holds nothing for me,' will be stuck in my head forever.

"And at Saddleback, where you're basically at ground zero for American wealth and prosperity, the words on the PowerPoint 'Don't give up' just made no sense.

"That said, I'm just enjoying the songs more here, even though the call to belief in the words is the same as we've seen elsewhere: 'We worship you . . . hallelujah.' But these folks are singing these words with abandon, real feeling. And I think that if you *do* worship God and you are in the literal *act* of worshipping God, you are giving yourself over to a higher power which, in my opinion, should be done with abandon. The last thing you should be doing is worrying about your singing voice."

"But don't you think it's more a cultural thing you're talking about than a measure of belief?" I asked Casper. "Surely you don't mean that people who choose to express their beliefs in a more quiet, conservative manner are less valid than what we're seeing here? Do you?"

"No. I mean, I know that's not fair. Upper-middle-class people in Orange County will certainly behave differently than poorer people in the inner city of Chicago. But here, although the lyrical content is much like what we've heard elsewhere—in fact, I'm pretty sure this song is one we've heard elsewhere—something different is happening. It's getting into my bones. Jim, I have a confession to make: I think I want to dance."

"I'm not sure an atheist is allowed to dance in church without first surrendering his objectivity card," I joked.

Casper didn't get up and dance, but if he had, he wouldn't have been alone: The entire congregation was on its feet.

Soon Coach Gordon was starting to preach about what it means to never, never, never give up—a quote Gordon attributed to Winston Churchill. But very quickly, he deftly linked Churchill's maxim to Chicago icon Michael Jordan. Coach related how "MJ" was cut from his school basketball team in the eighth grade, but he didn't give up . . . and we all know what happened after that.

And with that relevant, hometown reference to His Airness, the crowd was all Coach Gordon's.

Once Gordon was finished, I turned to Casper to get his take on the sermon.

"What did you think, Casper? Well done?"

"Absolutely, Jim. He is really, *really* getting some work done.

Too often what I've seen thus far is pastors being focused on one thing: saving souls. But as I currently don't believe there's a soul, that particular act means as much to me as saving hobbits. But this guy I get. I mean, he's saving *people*. And he's doing it right in front of all of us."

"What do you mean? What are you seeing?"

"When Coach invited that guy Jason Little up to the platform, he was putting those words into practice. Jason's was the story of the day. Here's a guy who failed the eighth grade—was almost forced to quit school before he could shave. But he didn't give up.

"He reapplied himself and finished school. Then he took a different turn, started running with gangs, got shot seven times. Doctor said he wouldn't walk, but his pastor [another pastor from Lawndale] wouldn't give up on him, so he didn't give up on himself. Now he walks.

"But more important, he talks. He stands up here and willingly bares his soul to a roomful of strangers. Jason presents walking, talking proof of the power of faith—faith in God, as he explained, and faith in himself, as he demonstrated."

"Casper, it sounds like Jason's story moved you in some mysterious and surprising kind of way: Am I right? How do you make sense of this story if there is no God? Where do you put it in your thinking?"

"I don't think it's my thinking that's the issue here, Jim. It's Jason's. I mean, Jason was telling us what worked for *him*. And it just so happened that what worked for him probably would work for every other person in Lawndale, if not for me."

"Well, sure, I get that," I said. "I know you're not about to have a conversion, but why would his story about how God changed his life move someone who doesn't believe in God?"

"Short answer is 'whatever works,' Jim. It was moving to hear a troubled young man talk about how he was not in so much trouble anymore. And he says he owes it all to God. But I know plenty of people who have been in trouble and gotten out of it 'thanks to God,' and then found themselves back in it.

"I told you the story of my high school buddy? He was addicted to cocaine, and one day he put down the coke and picked up the cross, got really involved with his church, the whole community, all that. And he said the Lord cured him.

"Then, about six months down the line, he started doing coke again and was *still* going to church—by this time he was even leading the 12-step group! And here's the crazy part: He wanted to talk about his problems with *me*—an atheist—because he didn't want his fellow churchgoers to get all judgmental on him. Irony of ironies!

"But my point is that, in my opinion, it's not necessarily *God* doing the work. It's the individual, and it's the people he or she chooses for support. My friend either lacked resolve, chose the wrong people, or did a little of both. Whereas Jason Little chose not to give up, and he chose Lawndale for support. He has gotten all the help he needs to stand on his own."

"I'm happy for Jason's success too," I told Casper. "But I'm saddened—although not surprised—by your friend's choice to confide in you rather than his faith community. I'm not 100 percent certain why he felt unsafe revealing his struggles to Christians. But let's say when it comes to love, acceptance, and forgiveness, the church could learn a lot from organizations like Alcoholics Anonymous that specialize in those practices."

"I agree, Jim. I think that kind of overcoming of adversity is very moving indeed, whether you credit God, the church, Jason, or just plain luck."

"But, Casper, just to keep it real, Jason didn't just give God a little or half the credit. He gave God *all* the credit. And Coach Gordon backed him up with some biblical parallels too."

"I totally agree that Coach Gordon did a great job using Scripture, integrating it into his call to action. As a matter of fact, this is easily the most integrated church we've been to, and I'm not referring to racial integration.

"This church integrates words (Scripture) with deeds with proof. Jason Little is proof. And so far as keeping it real, well, I see what you see too. It's just that where you and Jason give credit to a literal God, I support your *idea* of God. Which means that I support that you have found something that works for you, and I respect your belief, even though I don't share it.

"However, to someone like me who doesn't believe there is a literal God that we're going to meet someday up in the sky, a God that can't be proven otherwise . . . well, to me, proof of good deeds like they deliver here at Lawndale count more than anything. That's evidence that you are following what *anybody* can read in the Bible: Love thy neighbor, turn the other cheek, judge not lest ye be judged."

"So let me get this straight," I said to Casper. "You're saying that Lawndale is providing the kind of compelling evidence someone could reasonably point to as evidence of a God being active in and through people?"

"Yeah, Jim. I am. And I'm also saying that even though I don't believe in God, I see evidence of the *idea* of God being a good thing, a great thing, right here at Lawndale.

"This church hasn't proven the existence of a supernatural deity or heaven or any of that to me, and I doubt anyone ever will. But Lawndale *has* shown me how good following 'God' can be, and what a positive difference Christians can make when they follow the teachings and example of Jesus like Lawndale has."

"Preach it, Casper."

An ironic thing about churches like Lawndale is that because they have chosen to pour their limited resources back into the local community, many outside of that community have never heard of them.

Maybe we can help change that a little bit.

Defending the Space
From Strength to Weakness

Evangelicals have been taught to focus on the risen and victorious Christ. But in 2 Corinthians 13, Paul says that Jesus was crucified in weakness, and yet he lives in power.

We often forget the restraint Jesus exercised and the weakness he exhibited. Jesus spent the first 90 percent of his life living an ordinary existence so that no one could ever accuse him of not being able to identify with all of us ordinary types. Yet this is rarely mentioned. We skip right to Calvary and the Resurrection. It's as if his first thirty years have nothing significant to teach us. The final ministry years are the tip of the Incarnation, the visible interaction of humanity and divinity, but the first thirty years are just as vital to understanding what God looks like when he is living a life more like the one we live.

Defending the space involves embracing the ordinariness of our lives instead of pretending to be something that we're not. When we practice leading with weakness rather than strength, we let God be the strong one.

THE DRUMMER'S CHURCH

Jason's House

It was one of our rare weekends off from traveling around the country, and I asked Casper what he was going to do.

"I'm going to church, actually."

"No kidding! Have you found God after all this?"

He replied in kind: "Yeah, Jim. That's right. I found God. But my visit this weekend won't be to a church with a steeple or any other traditional house of God, but to Jason's house."

Ah, just like I asked him to do. As mentioned earlier, it was Casper's friendship with Jason, who leads a missional community in San Diego (and who also played drums in Casper's band) that led to Casper's and my getting together in the first place.

Initially Jason was reluctant to let us use his real name in the book. He spelled out his reasons to Casper and me one night over pizza.

"I guess the main reason I don't want my name used is that I know how some people will react to my relationship with Casper."

Casper looked askance. "Are you saying you can't tell people you're friends with an atheist? That's ridiculous!"

Jason said, "No, no, it's not that at all. I just worry about people, well, obsessing over how I did it. You know, they're going to be thinking, *Aha! So that's how you reach the nonchurched, through this whole 'friendship' angle. I get it! I must find this Jason and learn how to do the 'friendship thing.'*

"And that's not what it's about for me," continued Jason. "I don't want our friendship treated like some technique, and I don't want to have to explain or defend or even be bothered by people who would assume that our friendship is some method of mine."

"Wow," said Casper. "That seems so cynical. Not of you, but of anyone who would think that friendship is a technique for reaching the unchurched. I mean, that makes for a pretty manipulative friendship, Jason, for both folks. The unchurched person is basically being deceived, and the so-called churched person is being, well, deceptive—not really looking for ways to be friends but looking for an opportunity to . . . to what?"

I jumped in and told Casper that the word he was looking for might be *convert*. And that there are many, many Christians who *do* see friendship with nonchurched people as a means to an end: adding more bodies to their church.

Anyway, Jason (his real name) relented after I explained to him that his relationship with Casper was so central to one of this book's themes—more and better open communication between Christians and non-Christians—that I wanted people to know that he's a real person. And using a pseudonym is not necessarily the best way to demonstrate openness, though we had some really good ones lined up: Mister X, Rudolf von Wertzenheimer, Captain of Industry, Pickle Butter, and on and on.

So for the first time on our tour, Casper went to church without me. But he was not alone at all.

"Tell me," I said to Casper, "what were your first impressions of Jason's House?" (And I capitalize *House* because, yes, he and his community have church in his actual home. Jason and his family live in an old Craftsman-style house in a working-class neighborhood not far from downtown San Diego.)

"First impressions? You mean from when I first met Jason or when I went to visit his church?"

"You choose, Casper."

"Well, let me give you a little background. When I first

met Jason at Outreach Marketing, I knew he was a committed Christian—most folks there were. Jason's day job there involved helping church planters, and he spent his evenings starting house churches.

"I remember the first time we did something social outside of work. We'd had a few conversations about music, had some similar tastes therein, and one day I said, 'Hey, want to grab a beer after work?'

"As I think about it now, I realize that I was testing him. Because regardless of what your belief system may be (unless you're a racist or something), if you aren't into getting a beer after work once in a while, well, you and I aren't really gonna hit it off.

"Not that I'm a staunch drinker who won't ever hang with a teetotaler—matter of fact, a couple of my favorite people never touch alcohol of any kind. But knocking back a pint or two once in a while is one of my favorite pastimes, and if you can't at least come with, well . . . long story short, he said sure, and we've been hanging out ever since."

Hanging out—such a casual expression but so filled with meaning. The term is reserved for the people we like and those we think might like us as well. That's what I want people to know about God—that God likes them and wants to hang out with them.

"All right, let me get back on track. What was your first impression of *church* at Jason's House?"

"Well, it was a gathering like any of the others I've been to at Jason's. There was food on the grill, drinks, people talking—some of whom I'd met before, some of whom I hadn't, about fifteen all told. And everyone was just hanging out. And yet it was also kind of weird."

"What do you mean by weird, Cas? Was there a different

setup? Chairs in a circle? Was a Bible being read? Were people holding hands and singing 'Kum Ba Ya'?"

"No, Jim, it wasn't them; it was me. I had a laptop. And I was there on assignment, so to speak, looking at my friend Jason and his friends differently, like some lab experiment or something. I actually kind of felt as if I was violating their privacy. Because they weren't gathered just to hang out, but to hang out and discuss Jesus, whom they see as the Son of God.

"And even though I don't share Jason's beliefs, I really respect and enjoy the guy—his friends, too. And I didn't want to come at them like a detached observer, like they were in my petri dish or something."

I asked Casper to tell me more about this respect thing. "Some Christians will read this and wonder how you could respect something you don't believe in. How do you differentiate between Christians you do respect and those you don't?"

"Jason doesn't have a big church or a million bucks or ten trips to Africa under his belt, but I see firsthand—almost every time we speak or get together—that he walks the walk.

"He helps African immigrants find their way around town. He and his wife teach English as a second language. He helps people build their homes (case in point: the kickboards in my house that I could in no way have installed without his help). He regularly opens his home to others. And he does it all because of his belief that Jesus is his Lord, and for him, this is what Jesus would have done."

"WWJD, Casper?"

"Yeah, but in this case, it's not just a bumper sticker."

"So tell me more about why you felt weird," I said. "Was it because Jason is your friend and you'd been there before when it wasn't a church? Like Mondays through Thursdays: house; Sundays: church?"

"It was kind of that, but I think I would have felt a little weird even if I didn't know Jason. You know the looks we get when we sit down in a church and open our laptops. I think it's because we create a sense of otherness by doing that: *We are not like you; we are monitoring you and your behavior.* And when you open your laptop at the dinner table while everyone is eating, well, it's kind of weird."

"You might be surprised to learn that many Christians and non-Christians have connections that look a lot like your relationship with Jason. Problems occur when Christians either completely hide their God stuff or they try to unnaturally sneak Jesus into every conversation. I think your relationship with Jason is unique in that you are both open with each other about where you are coming from and you've both found a way to be cool with it. You guys are 'for real' friends."

"Right. Is it supposed to be any other way?"

"No, Casper, it isn't. So anyway, how was the dinner experience?"

"Dinner started like any other dinner except that when the bread was passed someone whispered to me, 'This is Christ's body, broken for you. . . .' And when wine was passed, it was, 'This is Christ's blood, shed for you. . . .' And, well, I wasn't really ready for that. Communion right there at the dinner table."

"What do you mean? Did you think Jason's community wouldn't be into traditional Christian practices like Communion?"

"Maybe I did. We sat at the table, and I had a beer in my hand. I was hungrily eyeing the grilled tuna when suddenly out comes the Bible, and then a verse is read (from Matthew 26) and a humble piece of bread somehow 'magically' becomes the body of Jesus for them. And a glass of wine becomes his blood. The casualness was a bit surprising. But then I remembered, 'Hey, I am in church after all.'

"Each time the bread and wine were passed and they said, this is Christ's body, this is Christ's blood, it reminded me of the way my wife and I sing 'Praise God' whenever we have people over for dinner and sometimes even when we don't. It's just a way to make a meal more special, and the song could just as easily be something else."

"But you're doing 'Praise God from Whom All Blessings Flow,' Casper. That's a Christian standard. You might as well be reciting the Lord's Prayer!"

"We sing 'Praise God' only because it was a tradition of some dear friends who have died—who were Christians, of course—and it helps us remember them. But at Jason's House, people were humble before God . . . and never have I felt more like an atheist.

"There were babies, kids, young parents, young men with their girlfriends. Hands were joined. Heads were bowed. Eyes were closed. And unlike my family's tradition, this was not a tribute to long-gone friends or simply something to do before dismantling dinner. Bread was truly being broken."

"Sounds like that really moved you," I said. "What came next? Was there more 'church' during dinner?"

"No. We finished eating, cleared the plates, and then we all gathered in the living room. I thought, *Time for church! Now we're gonna do some praying and communing, and I'll get to see how the Holy Spirit thing happens on a smaller level.*"

Casper and I had already seen more than a few people moved by the Spirit during our church visits, and Casper often found it a bit "disquieting." He asked me what it felt like: Do people ever stumble while speaking in tongues? Do people make a conscious decision to raise their hands, or do the hands just start lifting on their own, i.e., is God making their hands rise? Is it only because they are in a room filled with other believers and want to show off ("Watch me out-Jesufy you!")?

I had told him that, as in any other situation, people are motivated to do what they do for all sorts of reasons.

"When people stand in front of your band and the whole crowd begins to wave their arms in the same direction, what's motivating them? Are they really doing it to tell you how cool you are or to look cool for each other?"

"I get you, Jim; it is hard to tell, but it certainly looks cool from onstage!"

"Right, Casper, and church is no different. We don't lose our sense of self-awareness because our hands are raised, and frankly, it takes a lot of courage to do it the first time. All the questions you are asking right now are the same questions that run through the hand-raisers' minds as they try and decide whether or not this is truly an expression of surrender to God or simply an attempt to out-Jesufy some of their fellow praisers. I like to think most people do it for the right reasons."

"Wow, I must say I'm not all that used to you defending Christians. Rather, I'm surprised to hear you defending a practice that I and many other non-Christians so readily associate with the megachurches."

"I know," I told Casper. "It's an issue that's personal for me since I've led hundreds of public worship events and thought about it a lot. But enough about me: Tell me why you were expecting to see some Holy Spirit kinds of activities at Jason's."

"I had asked him about it beforehand. I said, 'So do you guys, um, feel the Spirit?' He told me that, yes, they often do, but not in the more extreme ways I may have seen at larger Pentecostal churches. He said that people will sometimes be discussing something and someone will chime in with an 'impression' that he or she is getting. That's pretty much the extent of the Spirit there. I told him I can handle that."

"So what happened? Did anyone get any 'impressions'? Did you?"

"Well, not that I could see. To me, it just looked like people praying. But I did like the way they remained silent after a person prayed. I figured that was when they were making their direct addresses to God themselves, or maybe they were just thinking about something else."

"What about things we've been looking for in other churches, Casper? Was there music? Was a collection taken? Was what they stood for apparent?"

"Yeah, they did music, and that's when I started to feel much less like the 'friend who for some reason was taking notes,' and more like the anonymous atheist-observer guy I've been in all the other churches we've visited.

"A guy named Chris pulled out a guitar, but before he started playing, he said a prayer that went something like this: 'Dear God, this is how you've created us. I pray we don't lose sight of that. Let our lives and not just our voices be praise and sacrifice.' I suddenly wondered if Jason had tipped off his group to some of the criticisms I'd made about other churches: too much talking, not enough doing."

"Funny how we read stuff into the things that are said when we feel like outsiders, isn't it?"

"Amen! I mean, yeah. So then a song was sung—no PowerPoint, no screens, no string section, certainly no smoke machines or cameras—nothing but the song, quietly sung by a roomful of people: 'Because you were forsaken . . . because you died . . . as you my king who died for me . . . amazing love, I know it's true . . . it's my joy to honor you in all I do. . . . Jesus, you are my king.'

"Really, I was struck by the gentle presentation, Jim. I kept thinking about how it was at Saddleback: They sang these same words, yet they were less effective, maybe because it was less intimate. I couldn't help looking up from my typing to see if anyone raised their hands in the air.

"And then it hit me: This is the call to worship, so much like what I've seen elsewhere. I saw that everyone was singing with eyes closed, and I wondered why. To show that they are not communing so much with each other but with God? I wondered what a passerby might think: *What are those weirdos doing in there? And why is that guy taking notes?*

"And then, just like everywhere else, the call to worship was followed by prayer. And—maybe because I knew everyone, or maybe because of the intimate setting—it took on an intensity I haven't seen or felt anywhere else we've been, Jim. The words were very similar, but the feeling was different. I could really see how deeply they felt what they were doing—these people whom I've seen in so many other settings—it was as if they'd just gotten naked in front of me."

I asked Casper if he thought things seemed so much more intense because he knew some of the people there or because of the size of the group.

"Well, I didn't know all of them, so I think it was more about the size of the group. After all, the bigger the crowd, the easier it is to melt into it. I lived in New York for years, and I always thought of it as a crowded place where you can be alone, where you can really be anonymous. But in a small group like Jason's House, your cards are on the table.

"They talked about how they could continue to connect with each other and with God as their group grew from six people to fifteen people. At most churches, that's no problem: 'We'll just build a stadium and put everything on PowerPoint.'

"But here, this was a problem. Jason once told me that he thought the ideal size for a church would be about ten people. That way, there would be enough for them to make a difference in the community but not so many that they would become disconnected. And I have to say, I really related to that."

"So they did Communion and a call to worship. How did they do the rest of church?"

"That's exactly how I put it, Jim. Before dinner, I asked one guy I knew, 'So, what happens when you guys do church?' He said that it was basically a chance to get really, really deep with each other. I said, 'Yeah, but with a cosmic deity, too, right?' He said, casually, but with undeniable conviction, 'Yup.'

"But, though they prayed, they mostly spoke to each other. So, Jim, what do you think? Are they communing more with each other or with God? And does that matter?

"I think that the best way to start a conversation with an outsider like me is to talk to that person first. Don't leap right into talking to the man upstairs. It seems like most churches are not communities at all because there's hardly anybody 'communing' with each other. There's a pastor talking at them, and occasionally they bow their heads while he prays at, or for, them."

"Well, Casper, we actually *are* communing with each other,"

I said. "It is very much a community experience, and I can tell you from firsthand experience that it can be very real and very cool."

"Well, sure," said Casper. "I know what it's like to be part of a crowd that's grooving on the same thing, kind of like a rock concert. But how is sitting in church any different than that? I mean, watch the videos! Concerts and whatnot sometimes look identical to some of the praise and worship stuff Time Warner pitches on TV."

"I know, Casper. I wish I had a good answer for you. I can only tell you that I believe there's a difference and that I have experienced the difference, and leave it at that. But it sounds like you kind of experienced it yourself, secondhand anyway, at Jason's House."

"Yeah. I saw others experiencing a combination of community with each other and with something larger, too. And I'm not too sure I've really seen that anywhere else. Maybe it's just because of the intimate distance we kept at Jason's House that this sense of community became a sense of communion. For me anyway, that kind of connection is tougher to come by in bigger groups. You know how in a big city people walk with heads down but in a small town they say hi? It's something like that."

I asked Casper what they do about money at Jason's House.

"As you know, Jason works full-time and doesn't take any money from his church. But they did do a donation of sorts."

"How so?"

"They talked about what they were going to do with their time to help others and make a difference in the neighborhood."

"Like what? How are they connected with—or serving—their neighborhood?"

"Well, I know that they volunteer time with various human

rights organizations, and they also set up community get-togethers where they invite people who are not part of Jason's House, the church, to Jason's house, the home, to learn more about how they can help the homeless in San Diego. I actually attended a couple of the meetings they sponsored with the larger community.

"At one, they brought in an older woman who was petitioning the city to help the homeless in practical ways by offering public bathrooms. She said the homeless can't even start to get ahead without cleaning up, and explained how this was a critical step to restoring their self-respect and reassimilating them into society. I later learned she was a Quaker. But she mentioned nothing about her religion as she told us about the problems the homeless face, how she's helping, and how we can help.

"And the other time, Jason showed a movie about racism. But it wasn't some contrived film about how racism is wrong and we shouldn't participate in it. It showed people having an honest discussion about how people of different races make them feel. Which I also found effective. Because that tired, knee-jerk liberal message—we're all equal, we're all the same—is bull as far as I'm concerned. We're all *very* different. Let's talk about those differences and what we can do to better navigate them and make the world a better place."

"So it sounds like Jason and his community are serving their neighborhood in more subtle ways. I think we Christians often think the way to serve our fellow humans is by *bringing them to Christ*. But Jason's House seems to take a very different approach."

"Yeah, Jim. They're just bringing people together. I guess Christ comes later if—in my case, anyway—he comes at all."

"Did you end the night feeling like less of an outsider?" I asked Casper.

"No, Jim. I still felt like an outsider. But a welcomed outsider. The thing is, believing in an all-powerful deity, and communing with that deity, is very strange to me. I often try to think of some parallel I can offer my believing friends—come watch me talk with dolphins or come to my house while we attempt to levitate my dog. To me, these behaviors are no less strange than their attempt to commune with an all-powerful deity.

"Although, while at Jason's House, I did entertain the notion of joining this church as 'the nonbeliever,' the guy who's just helping people. But then I realized that I am way too preoccupied, busy, and/or lazy to start really helping others. I think maybe I do enough by doing no harm.

"Anyway, since I'm friends with Jason, a guy who creates opportunities for me and others to do good, I'll get in on doing some good things sooner or later."

(An interesting postscript: Casper told me he ran this chapter by Jason, and Jason's reaction was quite positive. He also told Casper, "I'm gonna hold you to what you said at the end!" Yeah, they're still friends.)

EMERGING CHURCH WEEKEND

Imago and Mars

It was our "emerging church weekend," which meant we would spend most of our time in the Portland/Seattle area.

I asked Casper if he realized the most unchurched area in the United States was right here in the Pacific Northwest.

"I didn't know that, but I do find it a bit surprising. Maybe because this area kind of reminds me of Colorado, and as you know, they've got quite a few churches over there.

"But I think I may have unconsciously attributed all the churchgoing in Colorado to the 'purple mountain majesties' feeling you get when you're there. I'm getting that same feeling here—did you see Mount Hood when we flew into Portland? It was spectacular!

"And y'know, when I take in the mountains and the trees—the awesomeness of it all—that's evidence of the *what* of our existence. But a lot of Christians would look at this and see more; they'd see the *why*, saying, 'There's just gotta be a God. No way these mountains could have formed naturally via shifting tectonic plates and billions of years of bad weather—God did this. No way humans could be the result of billions of years of evolution—God did this.' Some Christians look at the very same evidence I do and say, 'God did all this. It's right there in the Bible.'"

"I know what you're saying," I told Casper, "but there are also a growing number of Christians, many of whom would identify with the emerging church, who don't approach it quite that simplistically."

"Well, Jim, regardless of what you believe—that either the earth was formed over billions of years or in six working days—the

Pacific Northwest is a sight to behold, even if I don't see it as God demonstrating his reality.

"But wait a second—if in the Christian view, wonders of nature are evidence of God's reality, shouldn't that mean everyone in this neck of the woods has much more reason to believe? Why is the reverse the case? Why is there such a dearth of churchgoing in the Portland/Seattle area?"

"I have no idea," I said. "Maybe it's because there are so many nature-related activities like skiing, boating, and fishing to divert people. That might be the short answer.

"And maybe because this is the last frontier to be settled in the United States, traditions are not as deeply ingrained, and people are, well . . . *different* than they are in other parts of the country."

We didn't have time to finish our conversation. We had planned to hit three churches in one day at this stop, and we needed to get started with Imago Dei's early service.

"Imago Dei. Now if there's one thing that'll attract outsiders, it's a name in Latin! What's up with that? Why not something more up front like 'Church of Today' or 'Modern Church for All Ages' or 'It's Hip to Be Churched'?"

I explained that *Imago Dei* means "image of God." "They are saying that the ancient God who made you in his image is here to meet you. And one thing you can be sure of: Emerging churches choose their names carefully."

"*Emerging* church—does that mean they're just getting started or they're just starting to get known?"

"Neither," I answered. "*Emerging church* is a term used to describe a wide variety of churches that, for the most part, don't want to be like the traditional or mainstream megachurches. And while they don't really reject the traditional beliefs of Christianity, they do reject many of its values and practices, some of the very things you've pointed out at the churches we've visited."

"Well that fits with what I found on the Imago Dei Web site. In spite of its antiquated name, this church looks to be one of the more contemporary churches we've visited. But contemporary churches also worry me a bit, as they tend to be more overtly involved in politics than, say, an old-school church like First Pres, don't they?"

I told Casper that another important distinguisher is that emerging churches are—again, for the most part—uncomfortable with the overemphasis on politics that has become a central identifier of the conservative evangelical movement.

"As you know, I have a lot of feelings about the current situation in our country," Casper told me. "And I've tried to not let that color my work on this book."

"We *need* to hear how you perceive the relationship between politics and Christianity in our country," I said.

"Well, Jim, in far too many cases, saying you're a Christian means that you're a Republican, at least to outsiders. I mean, no American administration has ever been more loud about its faith than W's.

"And now that I think of it, a lot of the people in power in W's administration remind me of many of the churches we've visited."

"In what way?"

"As I see it, at places like Saddleback and Willow, you only have to *say* you're a Christian; following the teachings of Jesus seems optional. It's the same with this current administration. It's Christian talk, but then the bombs get dropped.

"If I were a Christian, I would be furious that these politicians dared to associate with the church and Christianity. I hear a lot of God talk coming from them, like the seemingly obligatory

'God bless America' they end every speech with. Can't Christians see through that stuff? I mean, does Jesus condone bombing at all? Let alone the fact that innocents always die in war, what the administration calls 'collateral damage'?

"And y'know, Christians might find it perplexing to discover that while being born again won't eliminate you from my friendship list, supporting the mission in Iraq probably will. For example, when I first met Jason, I knew he was a Christian. And while that raised a few questions for me—Would he be overly judgmental? Could I drink or swear in front of him?—it was not a deal breaker.

"However, if he had been in favor of the war in Iraq, well, we would have had a real hard time being friends, Christian or not."

"That sounds somewhat less-than-open-minded, Casper."

"True. But there are some things that I think this world would be better off without, and this war is one of them. I support fighting terrorism, and I support the men and women doing their jobs in our military. But I in no way support the mission they have been sent on in Iraq because I believe, and have always believed, that Iraq had nothing to do with the horrific acts of September 11. So when I meet someone who supports this war, I just can't relate, because the events aren't linked.

"Okay, I'm done. There must be at least a hundred books on this topic that you and I alone could write. So shall we, for the time being, stick to visiting churches?"

I wanted to hear what Casper had to say, but I agreed that we should pick up this conversation later.

The city of Portland is replete with old buildings and funky neighborhoods begging to be gentrified. Imago Dei met in one of those old buildings smack-dab in the middle of one of those funky neighborhoods.

As soon as we got out of the car, we spotted the redbrick, three-story school surrounded by an asphalt playground.

"Just like the old days," I told Casper. "This is the kind of school I attended as a kid. Did you expect we'd be going to church in a school today?"

"No, and as we drove here through the neighborhood, I was about to say we were lost, but then I saw all the people walking in the same direction with Bibles in their hands, and I figured where there are Bibles, there must be a church."

We went inside and found our way to an old auditorium with a high balcony circling all the way around its perimeter.

"What a great building," said Casper. "It's straight out of the fifties. I half expect the Beav and Wally to be here this morning."

We found a row of seats with some extra legroom and settled into the squeaky wooden folding chairs. The room smelled like my former elementary school, and I began to daydream about what might be on the cafeteria menu—hot dogs or mac and cheese? Mmmmmm . . .

The old auditorium was packed with a couple hundred mostly young people, although about 25 percent of the congregation was gray haired. As we fumbled to get our laptops set up, the band wandered into their first song: accordion, conga drums, and acoustic guitar filling up the holes.

"Okay, Casper, first impressions of the music."

"I'm starting to know these songs by heart—though this band has thrown a few curveballs, and the musicians are nice and crunchy. (Crunchy, Casper?) Yeah, y'know: young, wearing sandals, unkempt . . . kind of like hippies.

"What baffles me as always, though, are the words. 'What can wash away my sins? Nothing but the blood of Jesus. What can make me whole again? . . . Oh precious is the flow that makes me white as snow. No other fount I know, nothing but the blood of Jesus.'

"Blood, blood, blood. Imagine if Christians heard a Muslim singing about blood all the time. I bet they'd get kind of freaked out."

"Good point. I really think that kind of self-awareness will become more and more critical for Christians as the world gets smaller and the center of Christianity shifts to Asia, Africa, and Latin America."

In spite of the lyrics, Casper seemed to enjoy the music at Imago Dei.

"There's definitely something much less contrived about the people onstage here. When you're under ten thousand megawatts of lights, with your hair perfectly coiffed and teeth gleaming, the whole 'blood of Jesus' stuff seems downright creepy. But here, there's something folksy about it. It's gonna be tough for some slick preacher to come bounding onstage after the vibe this band has created."

I explained to Casper that, unlike some of the megachurches we'd visited, emerging churches work hard to avoid titles and the whole celebrity thing.

"Everything is about *not* pursuing or at least *not appearing* to pursue their parents' values," I said.

"Whose parents and what values?" Casper wondered.

"One of the interesting things about emerging churches is that they're often started and led by young people who grew up going to the conservative evangelical churches of their parents.

"I think it would be just as fair to call them neoevangelicals, in that they hold traditional evangelical beliefs but have changed the way church is done. That's why they have those candles down along the front of the stage, the guy painting while we sing, and a more casual dress code."

I explained to Casper that in the 1970s and 1980s, evangelical Christianity moved from the fringes to the mainstream, and of course, raised the church's cultural profile in the process.

"But, like all movements, they lost something on the way," I said. "And eventually some of the children who grew up in those churches decided that there was a better way to do church, and—*voila!*—the emerging church movement was born."

As if on cue, the band finished its set, and the plate was passed while a video ran. Casper and I had become accustomed to this segment and waited for the "up with Imago commercial," but instead we got something much more interesting, something that showed a side of Imago that involved getting their hands dirty.

The video featured members of Imago—including some we had just seen onstage—working to rehabilitate a public park that had gone to seed. It was a place where drugs were sold and families were afraid to bring their children. But this small, dedicated team from Imago transformed it into what they called a Sacred Space.

"That was excellent, Jim," Casper said as the video came to a close. "They are going out there and making Sacred Spaces, and it's not about plastering a bunch of Bible quotes or getting in people's faces. It's about making a tangible, visible, practical difference. I get that."

This project didn't take thousands of dollars or a huge public relations campaign, either. According to the video, the only thing Imago did was donate time and effort—and a few cleaning supplies—and as a result, they transformed an eyesore into a showpiece.

Families returned in droves. A local woman said, "I used to avoid that park even when I was driving. Now I can take my grand-kids there."

After the Sacred Space video, I told Casper that I liked the freshness and otherliness exhibited here at Imago.

"What do you mean by *otherliness*, Jim? Is that another one of your made-up words?"

"Caught me again. *Otherliness* is a word I use to describe peo-ple caught in the act of following in the footsteps of Jesus. They're focused on others, listening to others and serving others in small, doable ways. In short, they're 'otherly.'"

"But why do you have to be a follower of Jesus to be otherly? I often help people in little ways—granted, not with as much gusto—and I'm not a follower of Jesus."

"Agreed, Casper. Otherliness can be practiced by anyone caught *acting like Jesus*, regardless of his or her spiritual or nonspiritual affiliation. You don't need to be a Christian to practice otherliness. In fact, many Christians don't practice otherliness at all; some actu-ally practice beliefism, or the worship of right beliefs."

"So you think beliefs are bad or unnecessary?"

"Not at all. Beliefs are part of life, but when we make them the central identifier of our lives, they can make us mean at worst and shut off to good ideas at the very least. I simply think Christians need to make a small change. We need to major in otherliness and minor in beliefs, that's all."

"Beliefism. Otherliness. Do you always feel the need to use such abstract words, Jim? Why not just tell me what you mean?"

"Well," I said. "That would take all the fun away! Speaking

of new words, what did you think of Imago's term *Sacred Spaces*? I thought it was pretty cool."

"That's a new phrase that I think is great. It gets their message across, even if it's not that overt. I mean, when the pastor talked about all of their hard work cleaning up the park and then said, 'Watch what can happen when the people of God celebrate the Kingdom of God,' I got it. And even though the language was not as relatable as I prefer, *their actions told me what he meant.*

"And it's a great way to help anyone else get it too. Think about it: What are you going to respond to? Someone getting in your face with a Bible or someone showing you that care and compassion?

"The pastor also said something that made me think of Outreach Marketing. He called Sacred Space a 'beautiful inbreaking,' which is just the opposite of what Outreach and many of the megachurches seem to practice. Imago Dei is not trying to get you to join *them*, so much as they're trying to join *you*. I really like that."

I liked that too, and said so.

"You've got some nice wordsmithing there yourself," I said. "*Inbreaking* is joining an existing community action, while *outreaching* is inviting them to join yours. Is that how you heard it?"

"Yes; in most of my experience, outreach only lasts so long. The first step is always pretty good, polite outreach: 'Would you like to come check out our church?' Then it's ratcheted up a notch: 'Have you thought about where you'll spend eternity?' And then, they throw in the towel: 'Have fun in hell, sinner!' Maybe I'm exaggerating, but you get my drift."

"Sure do. And you should know something about outreach. After all, you wrote the postcards," I said.

Then Casper and I were treated to a sermon from Eric, a thirtysomething black man who was the visiting speaker at Imago this Sunday. Apparently he had been sent out from Imago to plant a church in L.A.

Casper leaned toward me and said, "Do they really need another church in L.A?"

I told him that whether or not the City of Angels needs another church, that's what Eric was doing. And based on what he was telling us, he was doing a pretty good job.

"This guy is good," said Casper, "maybe one of the best communicators we've heard. And he is way into it. If his church isn't attracting people yet, it should. His point about getting involved in the city and its cultural activities really hit home, too. Saying, 'God was a gardener. He stuck his hands in the soil. . . . God has made us all gardeners,' was good, but then he followed it with something every sermon needs: points of relevance. I like that.

"When Eric was talking about giving, it was the first time I've heard it put in a way other than simply giving money. When he said, 'Giving isn't really giving until it *interrupts your lifestyle,*' that just made all the sense in the world to me. It's something I've been wondering all along: If Christians believe in God and heaven, then why have we heard so many of them go on and on about the material things in this life?"

"Good question, Casper. So what was the big takeaway from Eric's sermon for you?"

"I liked his stories, religious or not."

Casper said he especially liked a story Eric had told about a friend of his with "all the money in the world," who tried to give a hundred dollars to a homeless man. But the homeless man refused the money, saying, "I don't need that, you do. I'm free."

"That was a great, great story," said Casper, "made only better by that half-mumbled 'Preach it' from the audience, which Eric bounced off of with a 'You guys are very white, but I won't hold that against you.' I felt less like I was sitting at church than sitting with friends, telling stories. Very captivating."

Casper and I hated to cut our time at Imago short, but we had to hit the road if we expected to make it to our next church appointment, the five o'clock service at Mars Hill Church in Seattle. Mars Hill is ground zero for the newest trend in the emerging church movement, a church that keeps the style but dramatically changes the substance.

We got stuck in traffic on the way to Mars Hill, so I had a chance to tell Casper a little more about the church.

"Mars Hill Church is one of the fastest-growing churches in the United States, attracting thousands of young, conservative evangelicals who are looking for an island of certainty in a sea of unpredictability. It also attracts older evangelicals and people who are tired of easy Christianity or who want a place where their teenagers can hear the straightforward gospel and stay out of trouble."

Entering the building, we couldn't help but notice a number of paintings, large pictures of Jesus screaming in agony.

"Nice place," said Casper. "Impressive. Looks pretty hip, pretty well done, and like it didn't come cheap either. But what about those pictures? They're 100 percent Mel Gibson *Passion of the Christ*. It's like image shock—you know, like walking into Starbucks and seeing a large Confederate flag over the espresso machine."

Although we had arrived late, we hadn't missed the main attraction at Mars Hill, Pastor Mark Driscoll.

More than a thousand people were sitting attentively in the dimly lit and very artsy large warehouse, which is situated in the working waterfront community of Ballard, a neighborhood just north of downtown Seattle. This is a Mark Driscoll kind of area—blue collar, beer drinking, and uncompromising. Founded by Norwegian fishermen, Ballard has become more genteel as property values have climbed, but there are a lot of industrial buildings left to remind people of its workingman roots.

Theologically speaking, Mars Hill is positioned about as far to the right as it can be and still be considered an emerging church. In fact, I'm sure that many in the emerging church movement wonder why it's included in this category at all.

Regardless, Mars Hill and Driscoll are definitely forces to be reckoned with. Driscoll preaches a gospel that would make any fundamentalist proud. He is uncompromising in his approach to the Word of God and is unconcerned about whether his views make him popular or not.

Apparently, in his pre-Christ days, Mark was something of a pugilist, which makes it easy to understand his approach to preaching. He appears to have simply replaced his fists with his words.

Driscoll came across as smart and articulate. The camera projected him on the big screen—open shirt and leather choker. He was fired up, talking fast and animatedly; he likes his work and it shows.

"We are not here to pursue happiness. . . ."

Driscoll loves to shock. On this night, he was talking about the second-most revered text in America, the Declaration of Independence, and its guarantees of life, liberty, and the pursuit of happiness.

"When we choose our own happiness over glorifying God,

that's when we sin. But if you glorify God, then *YOU WILL BE HAPPY* [he said it that emphatically].

"How do you glorify God?" Driscoll pressed the crowd rhetorically. "If you want to glorify God, you need to quit being a glutton and skip that second piece of chocolate cake. You need to stop having sex with people you aren't married to. And you need to read your Bible *a lot*. Then, and only then, you *will be happy*."

"Sounds pretty straightforward to me," I said to Casper. "What do you think?"

"Well, this is the first church that has called out specific sins, which really seems old-school to me. At many of the churches we've been to, the pitch has been 'Jesus died for your sins,' not 'Stop sinning right now.'"

"Right," I said, "which is exactly the critique fundamentalists make of churches like Willow and Saddleback."

"Well, the fundamentalists should be happy with Mark Driscoll then! But I must say, even though his message is not at all appealing to me, his clear-cut approach has a certain attraction, being relentlessly direct and all. But am I the only person who thinks what he is saying may be entirely impossible for many sitting here to actually undertake? I mean, is anyone here going to skip that piece of cake?

"And regardless, what's still missing for me here—and forgive me for being a broken record because I know I've said this before—is that from my perspective, Driscoll is not really saying anything that's going to make the world a better place."

"But, Casper, when people stop doing stupid things, their lives often improve, as well as the lives of the people they're married to and even their children's lives. How is that not making their world, at least, a better place?"

"Well, sure it improves *their* lives. But was Jesus all about improving his life? In my opinion—whether or not you think he was the Son of God—he was about effecting change within *and* without. And too often, the change churches seem to be asking for is strictly personal. Jesus changed the world, not just his diet, right?

"What I'm trying to say is I'm hearing a promise of personal happiness through a series of things *not* to do rather than things to do. I guess you'd say it's a call *not to act*, rather than to act. Driscoll's pitch seems to be that to be happy and achieve heaven, just say no to sin. Is that in tune with what Jesus said?"

Casper always had a way of cutting to the chase.

"Yes and no," I replied. "Jesus told people to stop sinning, to be sure, but he also challenged them to love others, and sometimes his directions weren't as clear or specific as what I'm hearing tonight. Jesus said we love (which is the same to me as Driscoll's *glorify*) God by loving others."

"I understand that Christians believe Jesus was free of sin, but my impression is that he didn't focus on that. He wasn't like, 'Look at me! No sin at all! Be just like me!' Based on what I've read, his main thing was going out and helping the poor in spirit and those who were suffering, and instructing others to do the same."

"Yes, I think I could picture Jesus high-fiving you on that one."

"I keep thinking about Imago Dei. They talked about how giving should 'interrupt your lifestyle,' and how we can create Sacred Spaces, and I really get that. And frankly, because of those deeds, *I assumed* that they were not having sex with their secretaries or eating too much chocolate cake. Driscoll's persistent focus on avoiding sin reminds me of the old saying, 'Idle hands are the devil's workshop.'"

"You're good at these quasi-spiritual sayings, Casper."

"Call it playing to the crowd. At any rate, at Imago, their hands were clearly not idle; they were getting dirty, as they said: digging in and helping their community. But here, the message seems to be 'The devil finds work for idle hands, so put those hands in your pockets!'"

I told Casper that it seemed to me that Driscoll brings an updated version of an approach to the gospel that has been tried in every generation.

"Anyone knows that the most successful businesses are those that reduce their message down to a very simple pitch," I said. "Buy this toothpaste and you will get the girl. Buy this car and you will be cool. Eat this ice-cream cone and you will be happy. It is easy to decide whether you agree or disagree, and, most important, the pitch evokes emotion, which is critical to get buy in.

"And he clearly has had no trouble finding an audience. You may disagree with Driscoll, which many contemporary emerging-church people do, but you don't have to wonder where he stands, and that's probably what makes him so attractive to so many people."

"Jim, this is actually what I was expecting from all the churches: that old-time religion—don't have sex, don't eat too much chocolate cake, don't sin! Who in the Christian community could possibly disagree with him?"

"Well, for one, many women do. Driscoll is unapologetically un-PC when it comes to his beliefs about women not having access to the same roles as men, especially in church."

"But how's that different from what a bunch of other churches practice, Jim? I mean, look at the Catholics!"

"You're right," I said. "But that doesn't make Driscoll or the Catholics right."

"So is that kind of a litmus test for you, Jim? Driscoll thinks women aren't equal to men, so he fails?"

"Not completely. I understand how Christians disagree on a whole host of issues, like any group. I would say it is more the tone with which he approaches the topic. It's the I'm-right-and-anyone-who-disagrees-with-me-is-wrong vibe he gives off."

"Probably just the so-called street fighter in him spilling over, Jim."

"Driscoll also likes to talk about sex a lot when he preaches," I pointed out. "I suppose because it endears him to the college crowd and makes him sound like he's 'keeping it real.' I mean, we have been here for fifteen minutes, and he has mentioned something related to sex at least once every minute. And it's my opinion (one I have developed over thirty years of observation) that the frequency with which preachers talk about sex in a negative tone is telling."

Casper thought for a minute before he spoke. "Can't say I disagree, Jim. Imago Dei set a better example for me, the way they focused on what they can do rather than on what they shouldn't do. How can two groups of people that follow the same guy have such radical, fundamental differences? You all read the same book, but it feels like you're not even close to being on the same page."

"I know, Casper, I know. I'm sorry for the confusion. That's why you and I are writing this book. I think that, in many churches, it's tough to see the forest for the trees. We Christians spend so much of our time trying to get others to see the light that it never occurs to us that we may be living in a fog."

"Well, you can follow me, and I'll show you the light."

"What do you mean?"

"Let's get back outside and enjoy what's left of the day. For some reason, I'm in the mood for a piece of chocolate cake."

Defending the Space

From Beliefs to Spirituality

Jesus never intended for his movement to become part of the religion business, but it has. Consequently, when you ask people to tell you about their relationship with Jesus, they might begin with something personal, but they are also likely to add the name of the church they attend, who their pastor is, and the unique attributes of their belief system—all artifacts of the Jesus movement's misguided association with religion.

Today, a shift is taking place in our culture—people are more and more comfortable talking about their spirituality and less and less comfortable talking about beliefs or religion. This should not be an obstacle for followers of Jesus since he had no interest in religion other than his cultural connection to it. Jesus was constantly relating with people who did not hold his beliefs or practice the Jewish religion. He had a knack for keeping a conversation focused on spiritual realities without playing the religion/beliefs card.

Defending the space means we stop comparing their worst with our best, and instead practice bringing out the best in people's understanding of spirituality even when it doesn't sync with our beliefs.

COME AS YOU *REALLY* ARE
The Bridge

In an attempt to attract visitors, many churches have done away with the formal church-clothes requirement and instead invite people to come as they are.

But the Bridge in Portland, Oregon, has taken "come as you are" to a whole new level.

"Well, Jim, this church is certainly the front-runner in tattoos and, um, irregular hair."

"Yeah," I agreed. "My CliffsNotes description of the Bridge is that it's a church for pierced and tattooed people. Barbara [my wife] and I have been friends with Ken and Deborah Loyd, the pastors of the Bridge, for over thirty years. Our kids were in the nursery together when we attended the same church way back when.

"At that time, the Loyds had the little house with the white picket fence, and Ken was the principal of the Christian school; on the inside, however, they were really just hippies for Jesus. And Ken and Deb finally decided they didn't want to spend the best years of their life (doing what to them felt like) playing church. So about eight years ago, the Loyds decided to leave a secure position on a large church staff in Seattle and launch out into something they had always wanted to do, something that became the Bridge."

"Who funded them?" Casper asked. "You can't just start a church with no cash. Was there someone behind them?"

"No one was behind them," I explained. "They just decided to sell their house, pack up their stuff, and move down to Portland to start a church for kids who are disenfranchised from church and society. They took their own money, rented an old warehouse, and began their very tough journey of connecting with kids who don't trust anyone over twenty-eight."

The Bridge currently gathers each Sunday morning in a local community center right in the middle of an artsy neighborhood about five miles outside of downtown Portland. As we pulled up to the building, we could see that the local restaurants and shops in the area were already bustling, and it took a minute to find a parking place.

"This looks exactly liked you described it, Jim: a nondescript building in a wonderfully hip neighborhood, people hanging out talking, casual, comfortable. If I were just passing by, I'd want to know what's going on here—Is it an art opening? Is it a performance space?—because it looks pretty cool and pretty real."

I was relieved that Casper seemed intrigued. A gaggle of people were gathered around the front door smoking and hanging out. And there was Ken, shiny bald head, tattoos, and all, right in the thick of them. I told Casper that the bald-head trend really helps us old guys out since it takes people longer to figure out our age.

"You thinking about shaving it all off, Jim?"

"No, just a backup plan," I said.

Ken was clearly happy to see us—although I hadn't given him prior notice that we would be bringing our church tour to his place. He looked straight at Casper and said, "We've met before, right?" Casper said no, but later told me that perhaps the reason Ken thought they had met was because of the way Casper was staring at him.

"I was a bit hypnotized by Ken at first," he said. "He looks a little like a bald Lou Reed. And, you're gonna laugh, but I always thought Lou Reed looked a bit like my grandmother. Maybe he thought he knew me because I was looking at him with that profound sense of recognition. Like I'd look at my own grandmother or, should we ever meet, Lou Reed."

"Too much, Casper, very funny. Hey, did you notice that not one *unusually friendly* person has welcomed us or handed us any brochures about the Bridge?"

"Very, *very* refreshing, Jim. And it gives me a chance to just see for myself what a church is all about before I'm told so by some brochure."

We went inside, and found that the church resembled something more akin to an outdated dining hall or an old Eagles Lodge. No altar, no crosses. Just art hanging on the walls and about twenty tables with eight or so chairs around each one, and food everywhere, available to eat in and to go.

The room may have been spartan and unadorned, but it was filled with energy and buzz. It was clear that people didn't come to the Bridge looking for a typical church service.

Casper and I were setting up our temporary press box in the back of the room—between the free coffee, bagels, donuts, and cookies and the take-as-much-as-you-want ready-to-go salads, fruits, and vegetables—when we heard a warm, inviting, "Hey you!" It was Deborah. Think Anne Lamott's blonde dreads, only shorter.

"What are you doing here, Jim? And who's this guy?"

"I'm Casper and you are beautiful." (Okay, he didn't say that, but Casper and I both commented later how ageless Deborah seems.)

"Deb, Casper is the guy I told you about. We're writing a book about church."

"Why didn't you tell us you were coming?" she asked, looking over our shoulder to see if the band was almost ready to get started.

"That's against the rules," Casper said.

Deb laughed and brought us up to speed on Bridge stories, which most recently included providing a full-blown, all-expenses-paid wedding ceremony and reception for two homeless kids who were seated only a few feet away. The husband was busily working on a laptop (turned out he had been, until recently, a computer technician), and his wife, who appeared to be about eight months and twenty-nine days pregnant, sat next to him.

"So, Deb, Casper is an atheist, which as you can imagine provides a unique viewpoint for the book on church that we're writing."

Deborah looked a little surprised. And then she surprised us by pulling what Casper would later call "a McManus," saying, "Oh, you'll fit right in here. We have a lot of atheists."

Casper and I started laughing (probably much in the way black people do when white people tell them, "Some of my best friends are black"), though Deborah actually counted and told me later that there were ten atheists attending the Bridge that morning.

And then the band began to rock (and I do mean that literally) the house.

It began softly, like the rumble of thunder over a far-off mountain. No Unusually Happy Announcer saying, "Welcome to the Bridge!" No giving of directions of any kind from the front. Not even a 1-2-3-4. Just a drummer beating out a tribal beat, which, unbeknownst to Casper or me, all the regulars immediately understood as the call to worship.

A few keyboard notes started plinking, then the guitar and bass joined in, and then the drums started really rolling as a second drummer (with a full set) jumped into the ensuing melee. The black-and-white words on the screen were barely legible.

"No slick PowerPoint," said Casper. "This place must have skipped the Willow Creek seminar or something."

The singers began singing, chanting, and—shouting. And the people—in the band and in the crowd—started dancing. I took a look at Casper. He was beaming.

Casper was appearing to connect here in the same way I connected at Lawndale. He was obviously getting into the music in a serious way.

"I like these lyrics: 'Your peace went deep beneath the deafening lies. . . . Your love came quickly and coaxed me back to life.' Maybe it's just because I'm digging the melodies, but the words seem a little more real to me right now."

"Words? This is more like a tribal chant!" I said. A large half circle faced the band, which was playing away at ear-splitting levels. But being an early pioneer of RLW (Really Loud Worship), I didn't want to admit that it was getting too loud even for me.

And then Pastor Ken picked up the metal thunder sheet and began to shake it furiously as the band crescendoed into a kind of tribal frenzy, culminating with a musical nonending—a fading away rather than a clean stop.

"Yeah, this is what I'm talking about: good songs played with real feeling. These songs not only appeal to me aesthetically, as in I'd buy the CD, but on a different level, too."

"What level's that?" I asked. "Would you say it's a higher level?"

"Of course a higher level. There's something about music and art that is not entirely easy for an atheist to explain. Sometimes, when I'm putting a song together or doing some writing, the flow kind of takes over."

"Casper, what you call the flow, Christians call God."

"I get that, Jim. But, in turn, Christians might say that God expresses himself through them, while I simply say that it's the humans' need for expression taking over. I do admit that I don't have a concrete explanation for the creative spark, how it feels when it hits me and how it feels when I see it in others, like now."

For Christians, the meaning of life can be explained in our relationship with God. But even though Casper does not have a relationship with God, he still believes that life has meaning. And as he freely admits, (and this is one reason why I enjoy working with Casper) an atheist does have a harder time coming up with reasons for *why* the world works the way it does.

I only wish that I could be as humble when it comes to admitting that I can't prove the things I claim to be true about life. For Christians, it is wrapped up in hope and faith and, well . . . a divine hunch. And yet I'm often tempted to act as if *I know*, when in fact *I trust*, and that is all that I really know for sure.

But Casper gets through life by working on his own and—by his own admission—"without God's help." And he does come up with "meanings for life"—good ones, too. In fact I often found myself nodding in agreement or sheer wonder at his intellect when he went off on one of his scientific method tangents.

However, in the thick of things at the Bridge, I think the last thing on Casper's mind was a scientific method or any other tangent. I got this impression from watching his head bob up and down and by reading his lips as he continually repeated the word *wow*.

"Something else, huh, Casper?"

"Yeah, absolutely. But I have a feeling the band's set—rather, the call to worship—may be ending. They did a rocker, followed by that really great midtempo number, and now we're into what seems to be a ballad. But I gotta say, it's not just the tempo and vibe of the music that I'm liking. The lyrics are a bit more immediate: 'The constant fight to believe / leaves me pretending to be free / I break out of it when I see / the same power that flows through you / washes over me.'"

I told Casper that all songs were written by Angie and Todd Fadel, leaders of Agents of Future, which also doubles as the church's house band. Both of them have been part of the Bridge since the beginning.

"Yeah, I knew they weren't from the same song factory that cranks out the tunes performed at some of the other places we've visited. Maybe that's why they feel totally nonmanipulative as they pull the heartstrings. The best way I can think to describe them is 'organic anthems.'

"So this must be why the kids come here. It's got to be that or the food. Maybe they come for the food, stay for the music, and leave with the Lord? Is that Ken and Deborah's plan here?"

I told Casper he could ask Ken for himself, since he had just walked up to us.

"Are you enjoying yourselves?" asked Ken.

"Ken, this is simply awesome," said Casper. "The music is real and really well done. The people are friendly and fired up. But how do you get them in here? Is it the food?"

"No, man. I just go out and talk to them, get to know them. They come because they like us. These people you see here today, they're not my flock; they're my friends," said Ken.

"All right, I get that. But we've been here for like half an hour or so, and it's been more like being at a nightclub than anything else. Do you guys read the Bible, preach, sermonize, all that? When does *church* start?"

Ken smiled and said, "It's already started, Casper." And as the music started to die down, he turned and walked to the stage, taking his place behind a lectern covered with band stickers, artwork, and writings. After welcoming everyone, the very next thing he did was invite people—anyone—to take the mike and tell us what they were thankful for, no conditions, no restrictions.

People got up and said how much they loved this church and how much they loved Jesus and just talked about what they were thankful for in general. It went from everyday kinds of things—going for a jog, hiking in Yosemite Park—to much more profound things. A mom with bobbed gray hair, one of the few "straights" in the church, stood up and said she was thankful because "I have friends who love my kids more than I could ever love them." A loaded statement, to be sure.

Next, the ratty-haired bass player dressed in a rock-industry standard, worn-out yellow T-shirt took the mike from Ken and said, "I'm thankful for a church that is more than a subculture—we serve those outside and come here to get healed up."

Ken put his arms around the guy's shoulder and said, "This guy left for a month and we didn't know where he was." And then, turning to face the guy, he said, "If you leave again, we will hunt you down and drag you back." The audience loved it.

The last person to take the mike was a woman who said, "I've been lied to about who I am and what I am worth, and I am so grateful to have found this place and these people . . . everything we sing is the truth."

I noticed Casper seemed a bit put off by this.

"What's up?" I asked him.

"It's really amazing and wonderful to hear what a difference this church makes in these people's lives, and I am really enjoying myself, but 'Everything we sing is the truth' kind of makes me say hmm about it all.

"That kind of certainty always worries me. And this woman's comments were so strong—'lied to about who I am' is pretty big stuff—that her conviction that this is *the Truth* being presented here kind of strikes me as, well, fanatical."

I understood what he meant. I always cringe a little myself when I hear Christians make blanket statements like "Everything we sing is the truth."

"One of the reasons I am taking you into these churches is to help *all of us* see how we come across to people who are not predisposed to believe what we say we believe," I said. "I think she probably didn't mean what she said in the ultimate way, but maybe I only think that because I'm an insider. What I want to know is how statements like these sound to people like you."

"Well, in many cases, it's simply a matter of language. One or two words can make a huge difference," said Casper. "Believe me, I know. I have been a marketing copywriter for ten years. The difference between saying, for example, something 'helps you lose weight' and something '*can* help you lose weight' is dramatic and often the difference between a false statement and the converse."

I was beginning to think that we Christians may be able to keep our church doors open wider by simply thinking more about how our words are actually heard by others. We can't expect to change the church simply by giving it a new set of clothes; we need a new kind of language, too.

After the "open mike session," as Casper called it, came to a close, a clean-cut young man took the stage and began to talk about the Bridge's mission and how we can help keep that mission going. "It's time for the money!" said Casper.

He was right (I was wondering why all the punk rock kids had left the building; they must have smelled this coming). But it was nice to be able to see where the money was going: It was going toward the food on the table to our left, to help the homeless couple to our right, and to the rent for this space.

"Jim, these are, hands down, the coolest collection buckets so far," said Casper.

The Bridge was using Batman and Spider-Man trick-or-treat buckets to collect the offering. You can't say they don't have a sense of humor in the place.

They also have an obvious sense of equality. At the Bridge, men and women are treated equally, without explanation or exegesis. Deb began talking as part of what we soon figured out was the sermon, which was in keeping with the lack of fanfare at the Bridge.

While Deb was talking, Casper and I both noticed that it was completely acceptable for people to talk with each other (in lowered, but not what you would really call "inside" voices) while someone was speaking up front. I couldn't imagine this happening in any of the other churches we had visited. The ushers would have been all over it.

Anyway, Deb told a story about something that happened while she was taking a walk recently. Apparently, she came upon some really cool retro advertising signs that were just rusting in someone's yard. And she wanted them. But instead of simply knocking on the person's door and offering to pay for the signs, she started scheming about how she could sneak back at night and take them.

"I guess I'm still a bit of a thief at heart," she said.

To make a long story short, she resisted the temptation and

instead had a discussion with God about what was in her heart. She did this as a way of setting up the Bible story she wanted to talk about: the story of Gideon.

But she didn't read the story of Gideon for the people at the Bridge that day. Instead, she told them to read the passage together at their tables and discuss it, and she would ask for their feedback in about ten minutes.

"That is so cool!" Casper exclaimed.

"How's that?" I asked. To me it seemed a little, well, traditional, especially for someplace as hip as the Bridge. "Don't you think this makes it feel kind of like it's a classroom?"

"Well, yeah, but isn't that the point of church? To teach people? I mean, at so many churches we've visited, verses from the Bible are read *at* the congregation: Here are the words; you listen.

"But here, the Bible is being used as a conversation starter, to get people talking *with* each other. And I think it's only in these kinds of discussions—whether they're one-on-one or in small groups—where you can really connect or really learn anything at all."

"So are you saying that at a megachurch, it's impossible to connect to God? It seems like you're saying that the larger a church grows, the more difficult it is to keep people connected, and not only to God but to each other."

"I hate to simplify it like that, but yes," he responded. "Think about it: How do schools sell themselves? By class size. The lower the student/teacher ratio is, the smaller the class size, the better the education. It's because you get more interaction with 'the expert,' and more interaction with your classmates.

"Why do churches seem to do just the opposite? Why is a church deemed successful by its size rather than its ability to truly teach its people?"

"What about the small groups that churches—even the megas—offer? Does that address your concern?"

"A bit. But it seems that those groups, which I know can be very effective, are taking second stage—literally and figuratively— to a massive light show for a sea of people in a sports arena or opera house. Correct me if I'm wrong, Jim, but Jesus chose to have twelve disciples, not twenty thousand."

"Yes, Casper, your numbers are correct. Now check the numbers on your watch. Because although I know you could stay here all day, we've got to catch a plane and move on to our next church."

"Let's do it, Jim."

OSTEEN LIVE!
Lakewood

Flying into Houston to meet Casper, I realized that this would be my last weekend traveling with him.

We had been spending almost every weekend together for the past two months visiting churches all over the United States. This weekend in Houston and Dallas would wrap up our church tour. *What a blast this project has been,* I thought as I stared out the exit-row window.

George Bush International Airport stretched out below, and I felt sad that our visits were coming to a close. I also had a deep sense of gratitude for this opportunity, and I whispered a prayer of thanks.

Casper and I, a thirty-seven-year-old atheist and a fifty-nine-year-old Christian, a marketing copywriter and an ex-pastor/housepainter, writing a book together that we hoped would help to make the church a better place. Who could have imagined this? This had been too much fun.

"Hey, Jim! Over here." Casper gave me a shout-out from a café in the airport. Like two teammates eager to play the game one more time, Casper and I shook hands and made our way to the Alamo car-rental counter (yes, we chose it for that reason). Soon we were on the interstate, headed for downtown Houston and looking for another church.

But first, it was time to get some lunch, and Casper was insistent: "Gotta be Texas BBQ, Jim. There is nothing else quite like it."

We had time, and we had appetites, and we were in Texas after all, so BBQ it was. It was a balmy 114 degrees in Houston, and we found a BBQ joint that—lucky us!—only had outside seating. "Trust me, Jim. You won't regret it."

I have learned a lot of things from a lot of people in my nearly sixty years on this planet. I've learned that there is a God, and I'm not him. I've learned that some people say one thing and do another. I've learned that *The Simpsons* is a fine TV program. And, under a corrugated tin roof situated right next to a dusty Texas parking lot, I learned that Texas BBQ is a sublime experience.

"Did you just say 'sublime'?" Casper asked, BBQ sauce dripping from his hands and face, a mouth full of pulled pork.

"Sublime? Jim, we're in Texas! Saying 'sublime' could get us kicked out in a New York minute. And I still have about three pounds of pork to eat!"

After what was—no exaggeration—one of the best meals I've ever had, Casper and I went back to the car and began looking for Lakewood Church, home base of Joel Osteen, contemporary Christianity's brightest, biggest star. We didn't have to look very long to find his church. It was, after all, located in the former home of the NBA's Houston Rockets.

At Saddleback, parking was directed by congregants. At Willow, by hundreds of brightly colored signs. And here at Lakewood, by Houston's finest. "I think they may just be security guards, Jim. Regardless, we should probably have ID ready," said Casper as we entered the parking lot.

We got out of the rental and joined the underground parade. We were in the parking lot of the stadium formerly known as Compaq Center, now called Lakewood, with Joel Osteen.

Like a couple of newly born lemmings, we followed the pack through caverns of concrete that led us into "the big game." I felt as if I was making my way to section 10, row 23, seats 3 and 4 at a Seahawks game. All that was missing was the ticket stub.

Signage underground directed us to Lakewood and elsewhere. "C'mon, Jim! It's not too late to go grab a beer! How about it?" joked Casper. "Onion rings and Heinekens instead of fog machines and sermons?" He had seen that there was a sports bar here too, undoubtedly a holdover from when this was a sports arena.

We walked up the ramp, out of the parking structure, and into the center/facility/church/stadium, and promptly had our breath taken away.

The giant escalators, three-story-high ceilings, smiling people, maps, diagrams, and signs were simply overwhelming. This was not just about as big as church gets, this was about as big as *big* gets. There was a giant bookstore on the mezzanine level—I should mention that there was a mezzanine level, too—and there was just the general feeling that we were about to attend an Event.

"Who wouldn't be wowed?" asked Casper. "Look, there's even a human resources desk handing out job applications! If I didn't know better, I'd say we were at the mall, or at least at Willow Creek.

"Hey, did I tell you that I did some research? Last Sunday night, I caught Joel on the tube. Real, good old-fashioned televangelism, upbeat messages, lots of smiling people onstage, and lots of smiling people in the audience. I'll keep an eye out for familiar faces."

WARNING: I need to admit right up front that my perspective at Lakewood was skewed due to the fact that, as a young believer, God and/or my dysfunction saw fit to position me in the Pentecostal Church culture of which Osteen is also a product. Consequently, it's nearly impossible for me to remain objective. I simply know too much about this particular brand of Christianity.

I'll have to leave the more objective observations up to my atheist colleague.

Above us on the big screen, affirmative messages played on a loop: Discover the champion in you. . . . You're an overcomer, a conqueror. . . . All things are possible . . . all rivers crossable.

"Are we at church or some sort of self-help seminar?" asked Casper. "Being here in a sports arena reminds me of going to concerts, old school. I remember going to see the Who a long time ago, and today, I feel like we're here to see the Why.

"Let's get some seats up front. Oh, wait, it looks like these are taken." Casper pointed to the Bibles that had apparently been left to reserve the coveted front row. "Say, buddy, that seat's taken," said Casper, cheekily. "Didn't you see my Bible? That's *my* Bible, pal, and I can prove it: On the last page, the world ends."

As we found seats a little farther back, we continued to take in our surroundings. On the stage were enough risers to hold a hundred-member choir, and below was an orchestra pit that appeared to raise and lower hydraulically.

"Check the fog machine and light show running full bore," pointed out Casper, "and they're only rehearsing! This all really says something to me, Jim."

"Such as?"

"Such as 'Money is no object.' Every corner of the country has its thing, I guess. L.A. has its glitz, Chicago its blue-collar grittiness, and in Texas it's do everything twice as big. In this case, though, it's more like ten times as big. Man, how do people connect with each other in a place this size? It must be like trying to make friends in an airport. It looks like the bigger it gets, the more empty it becomes."

Up to this point in the project, I think I had been doing well at maintaining a certain level of objectivity. But something in me snapped while attending this Saturday night service. Lakewood and Osteen became my tipping point. As I sat in the telegenic center of modern-day Pentecostal evangelicalism, opinions that had been like wet cement suddenly hardened into deeply held convictions. Hunches formed over thirty years in ministry shifted like tectonic plates on the ocean floor of my soul. I was here to be an objective observer of just another church, but this time it was undeniably personal.

"Looks like it will be a small crowd tonight—the rain," said a woman (let's call her Daisy) to her companion (let's call him Bud) in the row just behind us. "Joel's been traveling too much. I'm about to go have a talk with him," said Bud. *Wow, I guess they do think of him as their pastor,* I thought. Joel had just gotten back that day from another weekend trip (along with the whole choir) to Sacramento, where they presented a Discover the Champion in You event. We'd hear all about it soon enough.

"You should get a job here," said Daisy. Bud and Daisy were reading the Lakewood weekly brochure that, among a host of other things, posts job openings at the church. Bud got up and went down to a nearby supply cabinet for some Kleenex. *It's like they live here.*

Then, as Bud sat down with his fresh pack of Kleenex, a PowerPoint presentation featuring announcements started to roll, and the house lights dimmed. Like frequent flyers, the insiders went about their business and routines, while the rest of us first-timers sat in awe of the light show, the smoke show, the technology, and the sheer spectacle of it all.

I leaned over to Casper. "I have to admit that I do enjoy the production," I said. "I put on events too, so I appreciate all the work and details that go into making things like this work. For my money, I'd say Lakewood makes the Dream Center look like rookies when it comes to putting on the show."

"Absolutely," Casper agreed. "But that's simply gotta be it. For whatever reasons, they have more money here. I doubt that the Dream Center would turn down any of these special effects and whatnot. And so far as 'for your money' goes, well, I don't think you—or I—could afford the lens cap on that camera on that fifty-foot crane. I wonder what their fog machine bills are?"

"You aren't kidding! Just the ability to fill this huge stadium with that fog effect is impressive. This stage show would make Andrew Lloyd Webber squirm with envy."

"Hey, she played something on *Dynasty*, didn't she?" Daisy had spotted a celebrity and was excitedly elbowing Bud.

We Christians are so ordinary, I thought to myself. *We talk like we're transformed, but like everyone else, we still watch too much TV and get starstruck by someone who "played something on* Dynasty.*"*

Speaking of stars, the worship band had taken the stage.

"I always wondered what became of Up with People," said Casper. A heavily made-up blonde with formfitting clothing—the worship leader—was absorbing the spotlight as Kenny G's Houston counterpart soloed in the background.

"I am blessed to be a blessing. . . . I have a promise, a promise of heaven." The camera did multiple close-ups of the worship leader as she lifted her hands, her rainbow group of background singers providing various worship poses for the crowd of about seven thousand.

The experience was like listening to a looping Hosanna tape or one of those tracks you hear on the Time Warner worship CD commercials. In fact, this church looked like the place where they probably shot those commercials.

"When I was watching Joel on TV last week and the camera panned the audience, you could see a lot of smiling faces, but I couldn't help feeling that—like Oral Roberts, Jimmy Swaggart, Jim Bakker, Robert Tilton, Robert Schuller, and every other preacher who, in my eyes, is in it for the money—Joel Osteen is a bottom-feeder."

"What kind of thing is that to say?" I asked. "Are you making some sort of judgment about these people here today?"

"No, no, not at all. What I mean is that Joel Osteen and other TV preachers are not making appeals to the worst people, but to the worst *in* people.

"They make appeals to people's greed, selfishness, envy, pride: 'You're gonna get rich, you deserve abundance, you're better than nonbelievers.' To me, it's not much different than what the worst of our political leaders do. Instead of talking honestly to people, they appeal to people's basest natures: greed, fear, prejudice. . . . I don't think it's a very Christian or a very American thing to do.

"But at least they practice what they preach: I mean, look at these brochures and handouts! Nothing but naked solicitations for cash. The call to action that's been missing in so many other churches is loud and clear here: 'Give us money. Lots of it. God wants you to.' What I can't see is what's in it for all these apparently working-class folks."

"Although many of these folks are what you would call the working poor, they can come and enjoy 'the Lakewood show' without paying anything," I said. "They get the music, they get to mix with the upper-middle-class, and they can even get Joel to personally pray for them if they wait patiently.

"And they get hope for something better. They get a taste of the good life. Which seems to be all you have to offer to fill the place up."

Casper nodded, then appeared puzzled. "Where'd the band go, Jim?"

The band had slipped into the darkness. And then there was a drumroll—not a literal drumroll but one you could feel in your bones. We knew it was time. Joel was approaching. He strode out to center stage with a smile that was blinding even from the cheap seats. He waved. The crowd, of course, went wild.

You cannot separate Lakewood from Joel Osteen. He could have a life without the church, but it certainly couldn't survive without him.

Joel quickly began to prove his value and rally the troops, who, frankly, didn't seem to need much rallying.

Such is the nature of star power in our celebrity-worshipping culture, I thought.

"We stand against the forces of darkness. . . . We rise up in our authority. . . . Thank you for restoring what the enemy is trying to steal . . . helping us to treat people better. . . . We are victors and not victims. . . . We want to see you live the life of victory that belongs to you."

"What do you think?" I asked Casper. "Does this message appeal to you?"

"Huh? I don't even know. What enemy is he talking about? Who are the forces of darkness? What people are being treated better? A life of victory belongs to me? I thought other preachers played it vague, but this is downright blurry.

"I mean, it's a nice sentiment and all, but I don't hear any meat to the message. I think if you're standing and presenting yourself as a man of God, you can do better than vagaries. But maybe I'm just too demanding when it comes to a sermon."

But then we realized this was not Joel's real sermon—just his warm-up talk. Next came Victoria Osteen, Joel's wife, to receive the offering.

". . . Your heart is being ripped out, but God can turn it around for you, and Joel and I and the whole Lakewood family are believing with you."

Victoria was crying—real tears, no less. The camera closed in. Her makeup didn't run.

"God, through your faithfulness to him, will turn things around."

For the first time in all of our church visits, Casper was livid, and I found it hard to offer a reasonable counter to any of his complaints.

But regardless of how Casper and I felt, the plastic buckets were passed. Meanwhile, the worship leader led the choir in an anthem of praise that built to several emotional peaks, providing ample time for the buckets to circulate the whole first floor.

And the entire time the music was playing, instructions on exactly how to fill out your checks remained on the big screen.

But really, what choice do they have? I realized. It has to take a good chunk of change just to pay the mortgage on this sixteen-thousand-seat building!

The choir earned a standing ovation while the overflowing buckets disappeared to some back room, and Joel came back to give his Bible message.

Joel Osteen is the premier peddler of hope in America today and via TV around the world. Everybody watches Joel. His stories are so simple and so accessible.

He is very disciplined and repeats himself like a politician, relentlessly sticking to the talking points:

- We need to go for stability.
- We need to be the same, day in, day out.
- If you are a moody person, that's a selfish way to live.
- Nobody likes moody people.
- Don't be moody.
- Your will is stronger than your emotions. ("Jim, how does that take into account people suffering from depression or mental illness?" I wish Casper would stop asking the obvious sometimes.)
- God wants us to be consistent.
- God will promote you while others get laid off (*if* you are consistent).

"Casper, tell me what in this sermon (other than your comment on depression) could an atheist, or anyone for that matter, find objectionable?"

"Right you are," he said. "It'd be like disliking the taste of water. It's so bland, how can it offend? By the same token, how can it inspire? Be consistent? Be stable? Why not say, 'Steady as she goes'?

"What bugs me more than its inoffensiveness is its ineffectiveness. How can people live up to this unless they're on a nonstop diet of Prozac? Don't be moody? I know a lot of Christians, and just like everybody else, they have their good days and their bad days. None of them are Joel Osteen consistent. I know I'm not.

"And what does any of this have to do with God or Jesus? I mean, he hasn't even said Jesus' name once!"

I told Casper that this is one problem many traditional evangelicals have with Osteen: not enough talk about Jesus. But I had a different problem with this double message that Joel seemed to be giving, and it permeates Pentecostalism and most all evangelicalism. The message goes like this: Stay consistently happy and in a good mood, and God will bless you.

But since no one can accomplish this, they don't get blessed. And when they don't get blessed, they have only who to blame? Themselves. They can't blame God because he is only responsible to take care of those who are consistent and in a good mood. It's this kind of circular thinking and, frankly, crazy promise-making preaching I was referring to when I said I had hit a tipping point.

Joel Osteen then asked everyone to stand, raise their Bible high in the air, and repeat the Lakewood Creed: "This is my Bible. . . ." Casper later told me he was pretty sure that this particular part of the service had been lifted part and parcel from *Full Metal Jacket* ("This is my rifle").

Joel said, "Do you receive him tonight? I know you do."

And then, meeting Casper's still-falling expectations and much to my chagrin, Joel added, "Do you know where you'd spend eternity if you died in just a few minutes?"

I assumed the cameras were turned off for this segment since the hope peddler was switching into the evangelist.

"Oh, man," said Casper. "Here comes the 'you're gonna die' closer. Can't these guys get more creative, Jim?"

Joel called the unsaved to "accept the free gift of Christ's salvation. . . . I don't want you to go home tonight without being saved." He asked anyone who was ready to stand.

"The moment you stood up tonight, God washed away all of

your sins." And with that, Casper and I stood up and headed for the exit.

"Well, Casper, how about a good old-fashioned rating on a scale of one to five?"

"He gets a five as a presenter, one of the best I've seen anywhere. Awesome eye contact, hand movements, elocution. No wonder he's so popular. It's like getting a clinic on public speaking."

"I'm definitely with you on that level," I told Casper. "What about the message itself? The substance of what Joel was saying?"

"What message? 'Be consistent'? 'Don't be moody'? Can anyone in that audience, or in any audience anywhere, tell me they've never heard that before? I could have gotten the same feel-good, keep-your-chin-up message from Ann Landers.

"Reminds me of some lyrics I heard once by a band called Refused: 'Good frames won't save bad paintings.' But in this case, good speaking won't save a bad message. It flat-out mystifies me why people show him the money. So as far as the message goes, the substance, Joel barely gets a one.

"And one more thing, while I'm on a roll. Maybe it's me, maybe it's going to all these churches, maybe it's all the infomercials I've watched, but I didn't hear anything that I haven't heard Tony Robbins say better. Nothing about helping *other* people, no Scripture that I can remember, and nothing really even about God. There were maybe a couple of backhanded promises of heaven, but they were always tied to a dollar figure.

"As you well know, I'm not a Christian. But if I were, I would be hard pressed to explain all of this to an atheist."

Defending the Space

From Debate to Dialogue

Debate is about humiliating your opponent. That's defending the faith.

Dialogue is about inviting your new friend into conversation. That's defending the space.

Jesus was a master dialogist (an expert in dialogue). He didn't use power to overcome; he used kindness to overwhelm.

Defending the space happens when listening trumps talk and reflection trumps reactivity.

KEEPING IT REAL
The Potter's House

We walked back to the car from Lakewood with our heads still buzzing from the show. We were both a little churched out. This had been our sixth church visit within two weeks. And we were just about to wrap up the last one we'd take in together, at least as far as writing the book went.

Casper finally broke the silence.

"My head is dizzy," he said. "So many churches, so many preachers, so different, so identical."

"What do you mean, 'so different, so identical'? Do you mean they're different in their approaches but identical in their mission? Because that's what I'd like to see."

"No. What I mean is that they all have basically the same form, the same basic 'set list.' I now know generally what to expect and in what order: the call to worship, the reading, the collection, the sermon. But they're very different in how they execute that set list: loud, quiet, big-budget, low-budget, no-budget, long, short, plugged-in, unplugged, and so on."

"Well, at least we're all on the same page," I joked. But Casper wasn't laughing.

"Not even, Jim. I'm only talking about the form, not the function. The forms of these churches are generally united, even though they may dress them up a bit differently. But the function—or the mission, as you call it—well, that's all over the place.

"The church's mission is to plant more churches, or the church's mission is to help those in need, or the church's mission is to make people into millionaires—or at least promise to—and make the church leaders millionaires in the process.

"I'm telling you, Jim, if this had been how we started the project instead of how we're ending it, well, you'd probably have a much more cynical atheist on your hands."

Casper and I were soon on the road, making the short trip (in terms of Texas) to the Potter's House in Dallas, home of mega-pastor and international celebrity T. D. Jakes.

The heat was on in Texas as Casper and I made the four-hour drive from Houston. It was still in the nineties at one o'clock in the morning when we finally found a Best Western to crash in just outside Dallas. Breathtaking lightning storms lit up the open prairie skies during our drive, giving Casper and me an opportunity to trade ideas and jokes about who or what to thank for the show.

Speaking of shows, the Potter's House gave us one of the biggest shows we'd seen on our tour. The Potter's House offers the energy of Dream Center, the polish of Lakewood, and the talent of both places combined. And the talent was not just musical; it was promotional as well.

"This song is from my newest CD, which is for sale right after the service! Church, just to keep it real, it would help me if you buy the CD this week because the ratings people at *Billboard* magazine see the first fifteen to thirty days as critical . . ."

The crowd cheered—no that's too soft. Actually, they *screamed*, and Pastor Jimmy Johnson launched into his newest worship hit backed up by an incredibly hot band and the ten-member Josiah singers.

"Told not just to buy it but when and why. There's a lot of 'telling' happening here," said Casper. "We were told where to park—by guys in combat boots with walkie-talkies, no less—we were told where to sit, told to shut off our cell phones, told to say,

'Hi, neighbor,' and now told to buy this CD in the first week it comes out so this guy can have a best seller."

I had already struggled with my own personal biases this weekend, and I knew I needed to deal with one more before we got too much further into the service.

"Casper, I have to admit something to you," I said. "I tend to give black churches the benefit of the doubt more than I do white churches. Maybe it's my music background or the fact that after my parents split up I secretly adopted Ray Charles and James Brown as my surrogate uncles, but simply put, I am most comfortable in black churches. So you're going to have to help me keep it real today."

Casper smiled. "Hasn't that been my job all along, Jim?"

Pastor Jimmy continued warming the audience up.

"I'm a psalmist and a musician, and the Lord has been speaking to me this past year to bring a message to the body of Christ."

"Bring a message to the body of Christ? What's he talking about?" asked Casper.

I explained that Pastor Jimmy was using a popular metaphor that the apostle Paul introduced in the book of Romans.

"Paul said the church was like a body and that just as no member of our own physical body is more important than another, no one person in the church is any more important than another."

"So everybody here is as important as Jakes? And everyone at Lakewood is equal to Joel? That may be what they're saying, but when the pastors go home to their estates and their parishioners go home to their apartments, I doubt any of them really believe it.

"Can you picture any of these people at their kitchen table, scarfing SpaghettiOs out of the can and thinking, *Me and T. D. We are of the same body*? It's gotta be something like what our soldiers must feel when they hear the president say, 'We're all in this together': Ummm, no, we're not. We're being shot at in Baghdad, and you're watching *Dancing with the Stars*."

"Speaking of dancing, Casper, I must get to my feet and do some worshipping." And I stood up and joined the dancing crowd of nearly three thousand.

Casper later congratulated me on my dancing: "Wow, Jim. And I thought the only time I'd get to see you bust a move was at the Bridge. Get on down with your bad self!"

"I just need to connect with God once in a while," I said.

I sat down, and Casper was done talking dancing. He had more questions about the body of Christ.

"If every church is of the same body," he asked, "then why is this megachurch all black and megas like Willow and Saddleback all white? The leading roles are reversed—with blacks in the majority here and whites making token strategic appearances. But why don't they worship together?

"If you follow Paul's metaphor, the church should be the most integrated place in America, but even I've heard the line about eleven o'clock Sunday morning being the most segregated hour in America. Why the segregation? Aren't you guys in the 'love your neighbor as you love yourself' business? I mean it. No other group out there preaches togetherness more than the church, and no other group out there is as obviously segregated. Last night, we were in a white church. Today, we're in a black church. And that's just how it is?

"I'm not trying to go overboard in 'keeping it real,'" said Casper. "But tell me why I should join a movement that preaches love and equality and one body but for two thousand years has itself essentially resisted the very change it preaches about? It makes a good case for being an atheist if the very people who claim to be serving God and obeying him aren't doing what they say he's telling them to do. What kind of a religion is that?"

Casper had a point. When it comes to issues of race, it does seem that Christianity has drifted quite far from the standard we like to preach about. We are like everyone else in many ways. We say one thing and do another. And if we weren't preaching about obeying God so loudly, maybe Casper wouldn't feel the need to put us on the hook.

"The bottom line is that you are right," I told Casper. "The church talks a good game, but if we are ever going to be the body of Christ that Pastor Jimmy and the apostle Paul are talking about, we have a long way to go."

And then, right in the middle of our back-and-forth discussion on race and the church, the Potter's House exploded in cheers.

"I'm sorry I can't be with all of you this weekend at the Potter's House, but I have just finished a big week at MegaFest in Atlanta with Kirk Franklin and the Queen of Soul herself, Aretha Franklin."

T. D. Jakes was up on the big screen, talking to the church via a prerecorded video. Even via video, his presence was felt. As I watched, I continued to think about "the body." If this church was a body, then T. D. was its brains, backbone, heart, and soul.

With the city of Atlanta stretching behind him, Jakes addressed the crowd from his hotel balcony, the camera zooming in on his face.

"I will be back next week with you in the Potter's House, the best church in the world." The crowd stood to its feet and cheered while Bishop Jakes ate breakfast in Atlanta.

"Let's thank the Lord for our visionary leader and his first lady—the bishop could be anywhere he wants to be, but he's chosen to be right here with us in the Potter's House," said Pastor Robinson, a T. D. Jakes look-alike, who was clearly reminding the church that Jakes was very important and they were lucky (or blessed) to have him as their pastor.

"Bishop? First lady? What's up with the honorifics?" asked Casper. "It feels like we're getting a little too close to celebrity worship. And lest you think I'm picking on this church, I'm not. I have been wondering about the celebrity culture in almost all the churches we've visited so far.

"Let's face it, Joel Osteen is a rock star. Rick Warren is an intercontinental emissary. Bill Hybels rubs elbows with Bono. I'm just not seeing the connection between these celebrity pastors and the body metaphor you are pitching me. As your surrogate uncle James Brown would say, 'Somebody help me!'"

I agreed with Casper that the celebrity pastor thing is garish and pretty much a reflection of the church's adoption of consumerism and technology.

"But take a look at how The Potter's House does fulfill—or attempt to, anyway—Paul's commitment to the body. If you add it up, all told this church spent about thirty minutes this morning recognizing the regular people that comprise the bulk of the body."

Pastor Robinson had acknowledged several groups of people who were having family reunions by asking them to stand: "The Jones family of fifty please stand; the Travers family of thirty and the Milton family of twenty, could you all please stand, and let's tell 'em that we love 'em, church."

"Pastor Robinson wanted those people to know they were loved," I told Casper.

I first learned about the importance of family reunions in black culture while living in Cincinnati. In cultures where just surviving is a mark of distinction, gathering the clan is a big and important deal. For people at the Potter's House, this was a part of their liturgy.

Others had been given their due as well. In addition to the families, the pastor recognized the deacons, the ushers, and many more.

"Tell me about it, Jim," said Casper. "He even praised the announcements!" Casper was right. After the PowerPoint ran with the announcements, Robinson had said, "Let me get an amen for the announcements!"

I pointed to a woman a few rows down from us. "See that woman down there?" I asked. She was dressed in a mixture of orange and pastels and was wearing a pink baseball cap.

"How could I miss her?" asked Casper.

"See how they allow her to dance, jump, shout, and basically have the run of the place (within reason)? Kind of like a free-floating cheerleader. What other church—besides the Bridge—allowed the kind of freedom to one person to do her thing as she felt the Lord moving?

"And before we challenge the assumptions that inform professional/celebrity pastors, here's something they *didn't* do that we've seen done in other churches: They didn't point out the *real* celebrities who were attending."

"That is certainly true," said Casper. "Michael Irvin [former wide receiver for the Dallas Cowboys] was right there, and no one was crowding him; no one drew attention to him. That wouldn't happen anywhere else, and I don't just mean in any of the other churches we've visited; I mean anywhere. But I figure that has more to do with T. D. Jakes than anything else. This church already has a superstar."

"I think it's more than that, Casper. I'm not excusing the

obvious celebrity worship that happens here and at many other churches. It's inevitable that someone who is as dynamic a personality as T. D. Jakes or as polished a presenter as Joel Osteen will have a higher profile and somewhat of a celebrity status.

"But did you notice that here at the Potter's House there is also an open welcome and support expressed for people who have been incarcerated? In most circles, ex-cons and celebrities don't really mix. So I guess my point is that even though we see them as 'celebrity preachers,' they remain in an environment, in the same room, and of the same body as everyone else from most every other walk of life."

"Okay, Jim. I'll give you that. So though the lines between black and white still may be a little too clearly drawn, the line between celebrity and average Joe, between millionaire and minimum-wage worker, is a bit more blurred . . . at least on Sundays."

Then, it was time for Casper and me to meet more members of the body at the Potter's House: a group of people the pastor called "professional ministry technicians, otherwise known as offering collectors. Casper was clearly amazed by them and this part of the service.

"The more you give to him, the more he'll give back to you? Waving their tithes in the air? 'Ministry technicians' with gloves collecting buckets and buckets of money? What an enterprise! I wonder how all these folks giving money would feel if they saw the room where the money is counted? You know they've got to have one of those paper-money sorting/counting machines like they have in the back rooms of casinos.

"And the blatant promise of financial rewards from God for giving cash here: 'prosperity, wealth, abundance.' It was like he was reading not from a Bible but from a thesaurus under the word *rich*. He did everything but put names and dollar amounts on it, but I can imagine it'd be pretty easy: 'You there with the green tie, give one hundred dollars today and you'll get $358 next Thursday from God!'

"But he was smart about it too. He said, 'Are you ready for millionaire status?' not 'Are you ready for a million dollars?' He said, 'God's getting ready to make you heavy with everything good,' which lets people picture what they want: a new car, a new home, new shoes, 100 pounds of ham—*everything* good.

"I thought Osteen's appeals for cash—rather, his wife's, since Joel didn't seem to dirty his hands with that part of the service—were fearless. Here, they're not just fearless, they're relentless and practically guaranteed! Does this offend you as much as it offends me?"

"I won't say it doesn't bother me, Casper," I said. "But this is where, for better or worse, my personal bias plays a part. It simply bothers me less in a black church than in a white church. We're talking about people who have been downtrodden for centuries. And now, when they have found a way to begin to assert themselves and acquire wealth, success, and power, it's my opinion that this bold expression of wealth and rewards and whatnot is also a public acknowledgment that they have survived and succeeded."

"I see," said Casper. "But since my assignment is to help keep it real, I'm afraid I'm going to have to counter that. To me, what's happening here seems worse than at some of the other churches. At other churches, they ask you to give to please God so that you may go to heaven. And if you believe in heaven, that makes sense. But here, they ask you to give so that you'll get rewards on Earth.

I don't like that because it reminds me of something more akin to a pyramid scheme."

"No doubt we have had more than our fair share of those kinds of money-hungry evangelists in both the black and white church," I said. "But the fact is that Jakes made and may continue to make a lot of his money privately through real estate investments. He is a successful black man with or without this church."

I decided it was time to change the subject and asked Casper what he thought about Pastor Jimmy Johnson's sermon.

"Did you like what he had to say?" I asked. "What do you think he was trying to communicate?"

"Well, I liked how he said it. He was the dictionary definition of a gospel preacher. And I couldn't help but notice his endless use of rhyme and alliteration: 'Your position overrides your condition. . . . Faithfulness is a prerequisite of fruitfulness. . . . Is this God trying to make me or the devil trying to break me?' And, of course, my personal favorite: 'Shondo, shondo, shondo.' That had to be tongues!"

There had been a moment or two where the pastor, as he himself put it, opened his mouth and worshipped.

"So you liked the phrasing and the pace, but what about the message? Did anything he said appeal to you?"

"It was certainly entertaining and was kind of like a Greatest Hits of Christianity: money, healing, answered prayers, and more money. The main thing he said—as I'm sure you're aware because he said it at least fifteen times—was that this is the year of the 'manifestation of the glory of God in your life.'

"And I liked it at first, because it sounded good, but then I realized I didn't really understand what it meant. Luckily, though, he told me what it meant. If I read my notes correctly, he said that the manifestation of the glory of God in my life would be through healing, my family—I must demand that Satan let my family members go—business, answered prayer, supernatural faith, and finance.

"He also supported something we've talked about before. He made up his mind about what he wanted to say and the pitch he wanted to make, and then he selected passages in the Bible that support that pitch. He even said it: 'I'm gonna extract various Scriptures to support the topic.'"

I told Casper that Pentecostal churches—especially the black Pentecostal churches—are known for being very up front about what it is they're doing.

"But cherry-picking bits and pieces of the Bible to support your chosen topic? I think that's like asking someone to understand the meaning of the *Mona Lisa* but only letting that person look at her hand."

"Keep talking to me," I said.

"It's simple: If the Bible is really the Word of God, it's very, very important to not take it out of context. I mean, that's a rule that applies to most every phrase ever said, so you'd think it'd apply tenfold to the Bible! You can't look at Leviticus and say God hates gay people, then ignore Jesus' endless commands to love each other. You can't take a snippet of the Bible out of context and misuse it, or spin it, to support your particular pitch. That's twisted.

"In my opinion the Bible is kind of like the Constitution: It's a document of the rules we used to live by and the rules we live by now, with each addition fixing and overruling what came before. Just like the Thirteenth Amendment overruled Americans' 'right' to own other people, the teachings of Jesus overruled some of the more, um, mean-spirited elements of the Old Testament. In my opinion, the Bible isn't a tool you use selectively; it's a lesson plan you follow, or at least it should be for anyone who believes that it's more than just a book of myths and legends."

"Okay, Casper, let me ask a question that requires more of your objectivity: We both heard the pastor speak about healing, family, and answered prayer, among other topics—"

"Don't get me started on the healing," interrupted Casper. "To me, that's just plain nuts. I saw nothing more than a little mob hysteria. [I'd say it was more like a group hug.] Is anyone who was 'healed' today going to stop using insulin? Throw away the crutches? Beat the cancer? That to me was nothing more than vaudeville. Because if someone could really heal by laying hands, then document it."

"I don't think that's entirely fair," I told Casper. "He was talking a lot about how God would heal what's broken in people spiritually. And as you could see, most of those people seemed to be going through something more emotional than physical. At least, we couldn't see a lot of people on crutches or anything."

"Well, Jim, one man's explanation is another man's cop-out. I think he said, 'Heal what's broken spiritually' to cover his you-know-what. That way, if people *still* have diabetes or cancer when they get home today, they can't sue. Sorry if I'm getting too cynical here, but that's what I saw and what I believe."

Casper had fulfilled his job of keeping it real even if it made me uncomfortable. He had experienced a wider array of churches than most Christians have in a lifetime. And he had done all of it with workmanlike commitment to telling the truth as he saw it. He had been a joy to work with, and his sense of humor was always there to remind me not to take the whole church thing too seriously.

Casper and I saw an opportunity to sneak out of the service a little early without bothering anyone, so we made our way out of the balcony, using the side stairs that felt like they would end in heaven, and then down the steps into the main lobby of the Potter's House, where we were greeted as promised by one final pitch: "Get Pastor Jimmy's CD—only ten dollars today."

"At least they're consistent, Jim."

We found our car one last time and headed back down the freeway to Houston, where we would be saying our good-byes. Casper was quieter than usual, so I asked him what he was thinking about.

"Well, this has certainly been one of the most defining experiences of my life, and I'm thankful for every minute. But here we are, a dozen church visits under our belts, and for every Lawndale, it seems there are ten Potter's Houses. For every Christian like Jason, there are thousands more who use Christianity like a blunt instrument to pummel people over the head with: God is great. God hates you. God loves you. God wants your cash. God will or will not let you into heaven.

"And the thing is, I still struggle with a spiritual belief system that pitches an afterlife as its brightest reward, its light at the end of the tunnel—whether it's Christianity, Islam, Judaism, Buddhism, Hinduism, whatever. Especially when that afterlife is entirely impossible to prove; it must be accepted on faith. Yet they talk as if it were a fact, and not just for themselves but for people who don't even share their faith! And facts can be based on a lot of things, but faith isn't one of them. Know what I mean?"

I could understand Casper's dilemma, but I wanted him to tell me more.

"Well, imagine that I started a company, and investing in my company and telling everyone how great my company is will pay off huge for you. I tell you to trust me and have faith in my company. I won't show you where it is or what we produce or who else works there. But give me the money and trust that it will pay off. You'll get rich. You'll live forever. Just have faith."

"I get your analogy, Casper, but at least Christians can point to the Bible and say, 'God said it right here.'"

"The Bible was written by men as fallible as you and I, Jim. To me, the Bible can't even be viewed as an accurate historical record, let alone infallible truth. Muslims have their Koran, Confucians have their analects, Jews have their Torah, Christians have their Bible. To me they are recorded histories and as such are defined by the mission of their authors. I am sure if Hitler had won World War II, we'd have a very, very different version of what went down during *that* time in history."

"So if heaven, an afterlife, an all-powerful God, and biblical truth aren't happening for you, what is?" I asked Casper.

"Personal truth, Jim. And people realizing that their beliefs are just that: beliefs. And that their faith is just that: faith. It's not factual, not visible, not tangible; it's just something they have chosen."

Casper had been around enough Christians to know how we would respond to these assertions. "I know. They'd say they're right, I'm wrong. God's on their side. But I would never tell them that their beliefs are wrong or their faith is wrong. Because I'm in no position to decide if someone's beliefs are right or wrong, so long as those beliefs don't involve persecuting or hurting others.

"I think if more people were willing to treat beliefs as beliefs instead of facts, that would make talking with each other easier. There's nothing worse than trying to have a conversation with someone who's convinced he's right. It's like the conversation is over before it can even begin!"

"I know what you mean," I said. "So if you wanted Christians to hear one thing, what would you tell us?"

"I guess I'd just like Christians and church leaders to be more honest. Not just with me, but with everyone in their churches. Stop treating faith as a fact. Call it a hope. Call it confidence, not certainty.

"I guess I'd like some straight shooting: 'Hi. Life is challenging. But we've found that being followers of Jesus has helped us. Maybe it could help you, too.' That'd be *refreshing*. And I'd be interested in hearing more and asking questions. In short, I'd be interested in having a conversation."

Defending the Space

From Manipulation to Intentionality

Everyone is in the conversion business.

You want me to like your house, your car, your music. You tell me why I should get a laptop or a cell phone like yours and why I would be better off if I didn't use artificial sweetener in my drink. You also want me to exercise more, and you know just the right diet and exercise program I should follow, and you also know for whom I should vote in the upcoming election.

I want you to follow Jesus and devote your entire life to helping others do the same.

How can we be true to ourselves and not lose our friends? How can we have an opinion, a point of view, and not become at best a pest and at worst mean?

To learn more, rent the movie *The Big Kahuna*. I think its content might surprise you, and it might help, too.

Defending the space is the practice of nonmanipulative intentionality.

IS THIS WHAT JESUS TOLD YOU GUYS TO DO?

I still think every pastor should send people out from his or her own church to anonymously visit other churches. The pastors—and the visitors—would certainly learn a lot, both about what works and about what doesn't work.

I also think that every Christian should be required to bring one cynic/atheist/unbeliever to church at least once a year (even if it means spending twenty-five dollars once in a while like I did). Doing so would allow Christians to see their churches through the eyes of outsiders.

Each church could keep a journal of these visits and post them for all to see on a public blog. In a church of seventy-five members, that would mean seventy-five cynics would be exposed to that church's culture every year and share their thoughts. This could lead to some significant improvements in how that congregation does church. I can't think of one reason *not* to do that—can you?

As you can imagine and have now actually read, Casper had a number of questions for me before, during, and after each church we visited. But the one question that was far and away the most difficult for me to hear was this one:

"Jim, is this what Jesus told you guys to do?"

Casper saw and experienced—over and over and over again—what Christians do when they do church. He saw it done with big budgets and no budgets, in large stadiums and in small build-ings. The same format repeated itself regardless of the setting. The greet-sing-preach-collect-present form played out in front of us with unrelenting predictability. And when it was all done, he would turn to me and ask, "Jim, is this what Jesus told you guys to do?"

Casper simply could not imagine Jesus telling his followers that the most important thing they should be doing is holding church services. And yet this was the only logical conclusion he was able to come to based upon what he'd observed.

If people who had never heard of Jesus wanted to see what Christians were most interested in, they would probably start their search in some of the same churches we visited.

"If that's where they started, they would have to conclude that Jesus' number one priority was that Christians invest the very best of their energy and their money into putting on a huge church service—a killer show, as it were," said Casper. "Jim, is this what Jesus told you guys to do?"

I'm guessing that a number of readers might think that I have not been tough enough on Casper. And I base my guess on the kinds of questions I get from Christians when I tell them about this project.

Christians don't like being in a "one-down" position to an atheist, or even thinking an atheist has anything important to say to us. Let me ask you, how would it feel to you if atheists were in charge, and rather than being called Christians (with a capital C), we were called christians? (I have to force my spell-checker to allow me to use the lowercase to spell *christian* but not to spell *atheist*.) Or worse yet, what if we were widely referred to as "non-Atheists"? That's how we think of them, and believe me, they know it.

You also might ask me why I didn't bring up arguments to counter Casper's sometimes harsh observations. Or why I didn't explain to Casper that there's a lot more going on in these churches than what can be seen in the church service. Why did I remain silent much of the time?

Three reasons:

1. I hired Casper to tell me what he saw, heard, and experienced when we visited churches—he didn't hire me. When we invite people to church, we typically invite them to the church service. Much of our mission lives and dies with how they interpret that experience. We don't get the chance to tell them all the good things that are going on unless we attend the rare church that actually talks about those things consistently from the front of the house.

2. Unless we're willing to remove the handles from the front doors of our churches and publicly say to outsiders, "We don't care what you think," the church must become more reflective and repentant about how outsiders perceive us.

   As long as pastors continue to promote "bring a friend to church Sunday" and as long as we put "Everybody Welcome" on our church sign, *we* are the ones who need to change—not our guests.

   Jesus gave *us* a mission. I don't remember reading anything in the Bible written to missing people telling them to "go into all the church." They don't have a mission to adjust to us; we have to adapt for them. It's called the Incarnation.

3. Most importantly, most ordinary Christians don't remember the arguments they memorized at the church seminar on how to win your friend to Christ. The fact is that no one really wants to argue, demand, or pressure anyone. Most of us simply want to know how to have a conversation with someone. And so, in solidarity with this silent majority, I chose to remain silent many times and not use the "special knowledge" I have gained in my training as a professional Christian.

Stage Time

Eleven o'clock Sunday morning is typically when pastors get to do their thing. They have been studying and preparing much of the week. They have been listening to God and people all week, and now they get to talk. It's called stage time, and they spend the majority of it on preaching the Word themselves.

In every church we visited, very important acts of service were taking place behind the scenes. Hundreds of ordinary Christians were serving the communities around them and sacrificially loving people. The problem is that no one knew they were there. They were given so little stage time (which as we have all come to know is reserved for *the* most important activities in the church, such as singing, praying publicly, collecting money, and preaching) that there was no time left for their compelling stories.

We may think we have such things covered by dropping them into the bulletin and the announcements, but tell that to the atheist who drops in, or to the seeker who gives a church about three chances before figuring out what the church's "thing" really is, or to the tired evangelical who has heard every sermon known to God and man and just wants to *do* something.

That leads to my basic question for pastors and Christians of all kinds: Are we in the preaching business or the people-changing business? If preaching for twenty to sixty minutes every week is as critical to our spiritual well-being as it has been made to sound, then why didn't Jesus use this method more often? Why did he give such short talks? Why are his conversations recorded in the Bible at all—as if they're on par with his parables? Why did he spend so much time listening to others? Why did he ask questions? Was it just to provide fodder for preaching, or might he have been providing us a model for how to most effectively communicate and perhaps even convince others about the veracity of his message?

Casper's question—Jim, is this what Jesus told you guys to do?—haunts me, insults me, and provokes me. We need to do better than this. We need to honestly admit that in fact, Jesus didn't care a whit about church services. He cared about loving and serving others and introducing people to a personal God who not only loves them but more important, likes them.

People need to hear the stories of everyday Christians helping others.

People need to see us put into action what we say we believe.

People need to be able to tell us what they really think of us and not worry about a fire-and-brimstone retort.

If we do such things, maybe we'd start to see a church more like the one Jesus told us about, a church that even an atheist might be tempted to be a part of.

Is There Any Hope?

I came to believe in Jesus as a young adult, age twenty-one to be exact. I was not raised in church, but I had a couple of near misses with God earlier in my life. In my first book, I mention that if someone had invited me to follow Jesus, I am pretty sure I would have become a Christian when I was twelve. I was that open and hungry—but the invitation never came. It never came because Christians have lost contact with the very people Jesus misses most.

This book is an invitation to hear what missing people think about us and about our churches. If we hear, we can change; and if we change, we can connect; and if we connect, we will find that even though Casper may not be interested in what we have to offer, thousands of others will be. If we will humble ourselves and learn from Casper's observations, we can make the church a more welcoming place to the people Jesus misses most.

CASPER'S CLOSING WORDS

"Are you any closer to God?"

That's what my mom always asked me during the time that Jim and I were touring churches. And I would always say, "Sorry, Mom. Not yet."

And that's still what I think: not yet. I had an exceptional time visiting some of the biggest churches in America. Like most people raised in the United States, I have been inside a church on more than one occasion. But unlike most people, I got the opportunity to attend church with an agenda. I was a seeker, but I was not seeking answers. I was seeking questions.

Jim was lucky (unlucky?) enough to hear those questions. And he often had answers, but he did not have all the answers. And that's really, really, *really* important. Because the moment you think you have all the answers, well, you might as well lock yourself in a cave, because no one you meet will ever have anything interesting to say to you again.

Certainty is boring. Certainty is closed off. Certainty is against new information. Certainty is a kind of orthodoxy, really, and it was those kinds of "certainty" moments—when I would hear a pastor or others in a church declare themselves absolutely certain of heaven, God's existence, truth—that I would get a little riled. Because being absolutely certain about something you cannot prove is simply dogma, and dogmatism is the death of ideas. And I like ideas.

When this was all done, Jim asked me, "What do you think about Christianity?" And I had a ready reply: It's a religion with well-meaning rules that don't work in real life. (Okay, that's not me; that's Homer Simpson.)

But I don't think I can answer that question because Christianity takes so many forms. It's like asking me, "What do you think about people named Dave?" Each denomination, each church, each Christian basically has a version of Christianity.

As far as the teachings of Jesus go, I love them. Absolutely love them. I also love the teachings of Buddha, Socrates, Teddy Roosevelt, Noam Chomsky.

The question that just came up for me again and again—having read more than a few pages of the Bible—is this: What does the way Christianity is practiced today have to do with the handful of words and deeds uttered by a man who walked the earth two thousand years ago?

There are some wonderful things being done by the people in Christian churches, of course: food being provided for homeless and helpless people, money being sent to the less fortunate, homes being built. But there are some incredibly nonsensical things being done too: light shows, services in stadiums, promises that "God's gonna make you rich!" You'd have to apply an awful lot of spin to any passage in the Bible to make the case for that.

Jim asked me what I'd say to Christians everywhere, if I could, and I think it's quite simple. There are two rules we must all abide by to live healthy, happy lives with each other and with everyone on the planet:

1. Be open-minded. Learning is the best thing that can happen to anyone.
2. Do unto others as you would have them do unto you.

And though I've never met the man, I think Jesus would agree.

Q&A with Jim and Casper

Rick Warren's Church

Q. In this chapter and others, Casper and Jim seem put off by "unusually happy greeters." Jim even says, "I silently wondered why we Christians seem to believe that it's our God-given duty to appear unusually happy—especially at church." How did Casper and Jim know that these folks weren't truly happy? Perhaps they seemed "unusual" to Casper because he has yet to experience the joy of being a Christian.

> **JIM SAYS:** I wrote the "unusually happy" line about greeters because I was a pastor for over twenty-five years and understand church culture. Whether those people were truly happy or not, none of us will know. The fact that we were "officially greeted" and then very rarely unofficially greeted was what captured my attention.

> **CASPER SAYS:** I agree with Jim. The people at Vons supermarket are always unusually happy and greeting me too.

Q. Although Casper is not a Christian, he does have a very strong moral compass. He places great value on people who practice what they preach, take action, and "make the world a better place." He also believes very strongly that the war in Iraq is wrong. In a world without God, where does an atheist derive this sense of right and wrong? And why is it okay to place a higher moral value on "action" than on other things churches are doing?

> **CASPER SAYS:** I believe that I derive my sense of right and wrong from my biological prerogative (I do all I can to make the world a safer place for my offspring—I mean, my kids) and from my parents, of course—nature and nurture in a nutshell.

So far as putting more value on action, well, there's a wonderful proverb: The road to hell is paved with good intentions. I believe in making the world a better place, and that can only be done through our actions, which—proverb alert!—speak louder than words.

Q. In this chapter, Casper is confused by the story of Pastor Tom's father coming to Christ: "Even when Tom told the story of his father coming to Christ, it was not about what his father did or how he emulated Jesus' example. The message was that you don't have to do anything. Just say a prayer, use the magic words, and you're in." This is the heart of the salvation message: We don't have to do anything—nor could we do enough, even if we tried. Why didn't Jim take the time to explain this to Casper?

JIM SAYS: Because I wanted his observations to stand alone and because I knew he already rejected our version of how one attains happiness through finding a personal relationship with Christ. There was no reason to revisit this issue with him. My only motive to include it in the book would have been to let Christians know that I know what they are concerned about, and that was not the purpose of this book. I also think that our simplistic approach—pray the prayer and you're in—is suspect when one takes Matthew 25 into account.

Q. Casper seems somewhat offended by the apparent wealth displayed in Saddleback's congregation. Why is that? Does he believe that wealthy people are somehow less worthy or can't be true Christians? What lesson ought Christians to take from this observation?

CASPER SAYS: I'd like to answer this with a quote: "I tell you the truth, it is very hard for a rich person to enter the Kingdom of Heaven. I'll say it again—it is easier for a camel to go through the eye of a needle than for a rich person to enter the Kingdom of God!" (Matthew 19:23-24).

And there was something said by the visiting pastor at Imago Dei that has stuck with me: "Giving is not really giving until it interrupts your lifestyle." How many of the neatly coiffed, SUV-driving attendees of Saddleback can say that they have given until their lifestyles were interrupted? If people who keep their wealth think they're going to heaven, I'd suggest they find a teeny, tiny camel to help make their case.

Church, L.A. Style

Q. Casper remarks that the Dream Center's parking lot reminds him of a neighborhood event, and Jim explains this as "the Pentecostal Church vibe." Isn't this simply the sign of a group of people who genuinely care about one another? Why would it be limited to Pentecostals?

JIM SAYS: It is not limited to Pentecostals. It is generally limited to people who suffer together, and the Pentecostals have an unusual number of adherents who would claim that as a bonding agent.

Q. In this chapter, Jim and Casper discuss the difference between Christianity and religion: "Jesus never intended for the institution we call Christianity to form into a religion." How can we know for sure what Jesus intended? And anyway, what's wrong with having a religion?

JIM SAYS: Jesus advocated the Kingdom of God—a movement. This movement became associated with what I have come to call the religion business around AD 300 through its connection with Constantine and the Roman Empire. From that time on, the church has maintained its identity as a world religion. Historically, many people agree with this decision, and many others disagree with it. I am among those who disagree with it because it has primarily served to institutionalize the Jesus movement. On balance, the historical association with the religion business does not seem to me to have been a good decision.

The Mayan and McManus

Q. In this chapter, Jim tells Casper that "we all, on some level, have a need to protect ourselves from authentic relationships." Why is this? And why does Jim believe that it affects Christians—especially pastors, teachers, and authors— more than non-Christians? How can he be so certain that people aren't being authentic?

JIM SAYS: Remember that this is a subjective book. There is no way I can tell you whether or not someone is objectively authentic since authenticity is in the eye of the beholder. This is my personal observation based on thirty-plus years working in the church and observing those we call leaders. The ones with the greatest gift for oratory are often the same people who lack relational skills. I don't know why that is; I just notice it.

Q. Following the service at Mosaic, Casper says to Jim, "We're talking about eternal salvation here, and if heaven is real, it can't be real easy getting in," but Jim chooses not to expound on evangelical works-salvation theology. Why not? What could it hurt to, at the very least, help Casper to better understand what he was hearing?

JIM SAYS: I have openly discussed the free offer of salvation and heaven we Christians claim to find in Jesus with Casper, and he is simply not interested. That is why I chose not to belabor the issue with him following the visit to Mosaic. I think many Christians who have ongoing relationships with nonbelievers will understand what I am talking about and why I chose not to revisit a topic he and I had previously discussed.

Mega in the Midwest

Q. Casper was obviously angry when his former boss tried to share his faith with him. He particularly loathed the manner in which this was done ("He threatened my life") and called it a "lazy approach" to saving souls. Christians would say that Casper's boss wasn't making a death threat; he was simply showing how deeply he cared for Casper—both in this world and the next. Why does Casper say this is a lazy way to save souls? The bottom line is that without Christ, we all face eternal damnation. There's no way to soft-pedal around that issue or make it more palatable—is there?

JIM SAYS: It was probably the dismissive tone his boss used, more than his theology, that got to Casper. Something else to keep in mind is that Jesus did not approach people who did not believe with the threat of hell, but rather the religious leaders, and he certainly did not allow all of his relationships with nonbelievers to be defined primarily by his concern over their eternal destiny. He was more interested in where they were in relationship to the Kingdom of God.

CASPER SAYS: Eternal damnation will not work on someone who doesn't believe hell is real. Although, in a sense, I do believe hell and heaven are real. As John Milton—who, along with Dante, basically invented our idea of hell—said, each man carries within his heart hell and heaven, and makes a heaven of hell or a hell of heaven. Do Christians show that they really care by saying, "Hey, do you have a minute? Do you accept Jesus? No? Okay, have fun in hell"? In my book, that's not caring; that's more like polling.

Q. In this chapter, Casper asks, "What do you think this enlightened, impassioned, and above all, humble carpenter from Galilee would say about Plexiglas dunking tanks, millionaire pastors, camera cranes, and music coming straight outta Branson? Is this what Jesus had in mind for church?" If he had to guess, what does Casper think Jesus did have in mind for the church?

CASPER SAYS: I'd have to say he had no church in mind. He had people in mind. It was always about people for him, so far as I could tell. These churches we went to—with the cranes and all that—had little to nothing to do with Jesus in my opinion. The people may have had something to do with Jesus, but it's tough to see in all the cacophony of the Big Show.

Q. Casper observes that for many Christians, following is a means, not an end: "Do all these people doing the following have any idea where they're going or what they'll do when they get there?" Most Christians would probably agree that being a Christian is as much about the journey as it is about the destination. What's the best way to describe this process—and perspective—to someone who doesn't share our beliefs?

CASPER SAYS: I think the best way is not to describe it but to live it. And to understand that there is more than one path to the waterfall.

Helen, the Almost-an-Atheist, Takes Us to Church

Q. While he enjoys the service at First Pres, Casper says that the use of King James English keeps the church from being contemporary. In much the same way that people enjoy a wide variety of musical styles, isn't it true that some people would be drawn to the more traditional style of worship modeled at First Presbyterian? Just as some people probably prefer Mozart to Casper's brand of music, some might prefer traditional worship over contemporary. What's wrong with that?

CASPER SAYS: I don't think there's a single solitary thing wrong with that. To each his/her own, in all walks of life.

Q. Both Jim and Casper observe that in many churches, the pastor ends the service "sounding as if he's about to cry." Rather than being insincere, isn't it possible that this is actually the result of a faith relationship that is truly authentic, emotional, and deeply moving?

JIM SAYS: I guess so, but after you see it repeated, you can't help but wonder. Everyone should visit four churches in two days and see what patterns emerge.

CASPER SAYS: Amen, Jim. There was no sincerity there.

Q. During a discussion about churches requiring their musicians to be Christian, Jim wonders, Who makes up these rules, anyway? *Wouldn't it seem inauthentic for a nonbeliever to be standing in front of the church singing songs of worship?*

JIM SAYS: If that is true, what about nonbelieving musicians? Many churches regularly employ them to provide the worship experience. How much farther down that road is simply hiring a gifted singer to sing some songs about Jesus? I'm not sure that most of us could discern the difference, given the high level of entertainment we have become accustomed to receiving each week. It would be interesting to do a test in churches and see if people could tell whether the worship leaders were really Christians or not. And if they weren't, and the worshippers still "met" God, what would that tell us about the worship experience?

Q. Jim's "just say hi" idea would eliminate ushers but require various church members to say hello to three people each week. When Casper points out that this sounds "canned," Jim claims it's a matter of perception, that having regular members make the contact feels more voluntary. Yet it wouldn't be very voluntary if it was an assignment, would it? And shouldn't church be about reality rather than perception?

JIM SAYS: It should be about reality, but the reality we experienced often left us with the perception that none of the regular people cared whether we were there or not. My issue is that we open the doors and put up Everybody

Welcome signs, and that makes us responsible to practice hospitality. The issue isn't intentionality; the issue is, why do we have to remind people or hire people to do this? What does that tell us about ourselves or our systems?

Big Church or Church Big

Q. At Lawndale, Jim wonders, "What if following Jesus meant something simple and easily definable and defendable to an outsider—like providing affordable housing to people all over the globe? What if that's all we did? Would that be so bad? At least then everyone would know what Christians did and what was expected of someone who joined them." But God created a whole world of people, each one with unique gifts, temperaments, and callings. Isn't it only natural that he would also want different churches with different missions and goals?

JIM SAYS: Sure, but what business are we all in? The obvious fact is that we don't all agree on what we are trying to accomplish, and outsiders like Casper pick up on that. They see the very same differences you say demonstrate our uniqueness and ask why we can't get along and make a significant difference together in our communities. What you may see as variety they see as a blatant exhibition of our divisions. Who's right?

The Drummer's Church

Q. Jim says that many Christians "see friendship with nonchurched people as a means to an end: adding more bodies to their church." But that's not really fair. Many people are more concerned about saving people from hell than adding to their church's numbers. True?

JIM SAYS: No, most Christians are not talking to their friends about hell because they realize that if they do they will lose their friends. Also, most non-Christians are rarely invited to attend church, and I believe that the primary reason is that many Christians are embarrassed to bring their friends to a place they think might judge their friends, which will again lead to a loss of friendships. For other ideas on how to connect with non-Christians in doable and human ways, check out my book *Evangelism Without Additives,* or *More Ready Than You Realize* by Brian McLaren.

Q. Casper says, "I think that the best way to start a conversation with an outsider like me is to talk to that person first. Don't leap right into talking to the man upstairs. It seems like most churches are not communities at all because there's hardly anybody 'communing' with each other. There's a pastor talking at them, and occasionally they bow their heads while he prays at, or for, them." It sounds as if Casper would prefer that Christians focus on people more than God. How does he respond to that? Many Christians would say that, while they enjoy communing with one another, they attend church because it helps them to better commune with God. What's wrong with that?

CASPER SAYS: I'd say if you believe in an omnipotent, omnipresent God, why do you need help communing with him? When a group of people comes together, it's typically to share in something, not to privately commune. And I believe Jesus spent time talking to others in order to effect real, lasting change. I don't think the point of his message was "come here, be quiet, go home." It was "get out there and help people."

Emerging Church Weekend

Q. Casper says, "Blood, blood, blood. Imagine if Christians heard a Muslim singing about blood all the time. I bet they'd get kind of freaked out." While he makes a strong argument about the differences between Christians and how we might be perceived by outsiders, he obviously does not understand the Christian doctrine of atonement. How are Christians expected to share their faith if they can't talk about Christ's shed blood?

JIM SAYS: I think his reaction was to how this sounds to a complete outsider. As insiders, we become inured to how our symbols and metaphors sound in the ears of others. Since the Muslim religion is taking a much more pronounced role in our experience, we as Christians now have the opportunity to feel what this fixation on blood sounds like to outsiders.

Q. Casper likes the way that Imago Dei "is not trying to get you to join them, so much as they're trying to join you." What exactly does this mean, and how can other churches learn to do the same?

JIM SAYS: We can find out what groups in our community are already doing to make life better for people and join them. Rather than start groups, we could join *their* groups. Rather than join groups to convert people, we could join them to connect with and serve people. This was one of the most innovative observations that emerged from our work together.

Come as You Really Are

Q. At the Bridge, Casper finds it "refreshing" that no one offers him a brochure. "It gives me a chance to just see for myself what a church is all about before I'm told so by some brochure," he says. What's wrong with brochures and bulletins? Without them, visitors run the risk of not understanding something that's happening onstage or missing an opportunity to connect with others, don't they?

JIM SAYS: This is probably more a reflection of Casper's personality, but I also think he expresses the postmodern mind-set. Many young people are tired of being sold and told, preferring instead to be invited and included.

CASPER SAYS: Hand out ideas because they can't be thrown in the trash. Brochures and bulletins are marketing materials, plain and simple.

Q. At the Bridge, Casper and Jim notice that it's completely acceptable for people to talk with each other while someone is speaking up front. They point out that if this were to happen at other churches, "the ushers would have been all over it." But is this sort of behavior really such a good thing? You wouldn't do it during a meeting at work or in the middle of a movie. Why should it be acceptable in church?

JIM SAYS: It was just refreshing to see that it could be done. I personally find it distracting as well, but I like the fact that it provides an atmosphere for people who are completely unfamiliar with church culture. I think Jesus would find it very comfortable.

Q. Casper enjoys the way the Bridge utilizes discussion groups rather than traditional preaching. In fact, he says, "I think it's only in these kinds of discussions—whether they're one-on-one or in small groups—where you can really connect, or really learn anything at all." If this is true, why do college professors still utilize the lecture format in the classroom?

CASPER SAYS: Well, I think that's a bit off target. After all, a college, or any school, is often judged to be good based on its ratio of students to teacher (the fewer students per teacher, the better). I would guess that some colleges utilize the lecture format because they're lazy. And it's an easier way to make money. But there's no better way to communicate or to learn than in a small group. After all, Jesus the rabbi had twelve students, not twelve thousand.

Q. Casper makes the point that it seems impossible to connect with God at a megachurch, yet each week across our country, hundreds of thousands of people attend large churches. How can he judge the relationship those people have with God (especially since he believes there is no God)?

CASPER SAYS: I don't think it's a relationship with God; I think it's a relationship with mob. Just like being at a football game or a political rally, you feel energized by the people beside you. And in my opinion, that's the connection that's taking place at these megachurches: "We're all part of this big, powerful thing."

Q. Casper claims that small groups, while effective, seem to take second stage to the "massive light show for a sea of people in a sports arena or opera house." But he only visited the light show, not the small groups, right? How can he comment on what he hasn't seen?

JIM SAYS: I took him to where people are invited to experience church. This is what is advertised, not small groups. This is where most of the money is spent, not on small groups. And this is where the public speakers, a.k.a. pastors, do their thing, not at small groups. If we want people to experience small groups, we will have to have a major restructuring of the modern-day church's values and practices. When they make it as easy and convenient to experience small groups as they do Sunday services, then they can cry foul, but until then church will have to live and die based on what happens on Sunday morning in the big room.

Q. Casper says that Christians' "certainty" often worries him, especially when those Christians claim to present "the truth." While we obviously have to be careful when we make claims, aren't there some truths that Christians ought to stand on? What about "I am the way, and the truth, and the life"?

JIM SAYS: There is a difference between certainty, and confidence or hope. As followers of Jesus, we put our faith in a set of beliefs that we choose to think of as real. We cannot prove any of them—that is why it is called faith. What bothers nonbelievers is when we assert that we "know" something, when they know that none of us can know anything until we die. I am very comfortable asserting my faith and my hope and my confidence that Jesus is God, but I will not say that I know he is God in the way I say I know there is gravity. I hope the story I have bet my life on is true, but neither Casper nor I will know for sure until both of us are dead. Atheists are very surprised when they hear me say this and wonder why more Christians can't admit these things. They are not offended in the least by my faith, hope, or confidence. I feel no need to try to prove that I'm right and they're wrong. All any of us really has is our own story. If we have had a real encounter with the living God, then they will simply have to deal with it in whatever way they choose.

Osteen Live!

Q. When "Bud" opens a nearby supply closet for some tissues, Jim thinks, It's like they live here. *Why is this a bad thing? If they "live" there, they obviously feel connected, which is what Casper's been pushing for all along, right?*

JIM SAYS: Nothing was meant by this comment. It really was just a passing observation. But it seemed amusing to see them treat a stadium like their home.

CASPER SAYS: To me, it seemed they were enjoying more of a sense of entitlement than of being connected to others. And if they were connected, it was to the place, not the people.

Q. At the end of the service, Joel disappoints Casper when he says, "Do you know where you'd spend eternity if you died in just a few minutes?" Casper has already made it clear that he hates this approach, but really, isn't this the crux of the issue for all of us?

JIM SAYS: Not for Casper and not for me. My life with Christ is now. I want to make this world a better place. I want to see Jesus' prayer answered that his Kingdom would come on Earth as it is in heaven. I want to see the kingdoms of this world become the kingdoms of our God and his Christ. I want the incarnate Jesus to express himself through me to the poor in spirit. I want to give a cup of cold water to a little child in Jesus' name and see the five loaves and two fish of my life multiplied to feed people who are looking to discover a God who truly likes them. Going to heaven is icing on the cake, and I expect Jesus' first words to me upon arrival to simply be "Nice try."

Keeping It Real

Q. The obvious segregation in our nation's churches concerns Casper. "Why the segregation?" he asks. "Aren't you guys in the 'love your neighbor as you love yourself' business? I mean it. No other group out there preaches togetherness more than the church, and no other group out there is as obviously segregated." This is clearly more than just a church issue; it's a world issue. Segregation is everywhere. What can the church do to rise above the culture and resolve this problem?

JIM SAYS: We could start by admitting that we have often been at the forefront of discrimination both in our nation's past and even in our own times. We could admit that we have been passive when we should have actively resisted the splits that occurred in every major denomination after the Civil War. And we could resurrect the heroes of the faith like William Wilberforce who led the fight against slavery for forty years and practiced a faith that integrated justice and devotion to Jesus. Those would be good places to begin.

Q. Casper claims that "for two thousand years, [the church] has itself essentially resisted the very change it preaches about. It makes a good case for being an atheist if the very people who claim to be serving God and obeying him aren't doing what they say he's telling them to do." Casper is making some strong generalizations and assumptions here, based strictly on his own perceptions. It seems as if he's expecting Christians to be perfect human beings, rather than the imperfect people that we are. What about those who do try to live what they believe? Don't they at least get credit for trying?

JIM SAYS: Sure they get credit, but who can deny his observations? We sing, preach, and even politicize our values. Who can fault Casper or anyone else for noticing that we don't live up to what we so loudly proclaim about experiencing new life in Jesus or being transformed? Probably if we were more open about our failures and sins we would be taken more seriously by our critics.

Q. Casper says, "I guess I'd just like Christians and church leaders to be more honest. Not just with me, but with everyone in their churches. Stop treating faith as a fact. Call it a hope. Call it confidence, not certainty." But faith is the very heart of Christianity. Jesus himself chastised people for having little faith; he also blessed those who had "great faith." Christians live by faith, not by sight. How can he ask us to downplay something so integral to our belief?

JIM SAYS: See comments above.

CASPER SAYS: Ditto.

Online Discussion Guide

TAKE YOUR TYNDALE READING
EXPERIENCE TO THE NEXT LEVEL

A FREE discussion guide for this book is available at
bookclubhub.net, perfect for sparking conversations in your
book group or for digging deeper into the text on your own.

www.bookclubhub.net
*You'll also find free discussion guides for other Tyndale books,
e-newsletters, e-mail devotionals, virtual book tours, and more!*

WHY **MILLIONS** OF TODAY'S MOST COMMITTED **CHURCH MEMBERS** MAY BE READY TO BOLT—AND WHAT TO DO ABOUT IT.

the **resignation** of **eve**

WHAT IF ADAM'S RIB IS NO LONGER WILLING TO BE THE CHURCH'S BACKBONE?

jim henderson

In talking with women around the country, Jim Henderson has come to believe there is an epidemic of quiet, even sad resignation among dedicated Christian women who are feeling overworked and undervalued in the church. As a result, many women are discouraged. Some, particularly young women, respond by leaving the organized church . . . or walking away from the faith altogether.

What does this mean for your church and for the body of Christ as a whole?

Containing personal interviews with women and new research from George Barna, *The Resignation of Eve* is a must-read, conversation-starting book for women who have been engaged in the church, as well as for their pastors and ministry leaders.

ISBN 978-1-4143-3730-2

CP0524